BY THEODORE ROETHKE

Collected Poems
The Far Field
I Am! Says the Lamb
Words for the Wind
The Waking
Praise to the End!
The Lost Son and Other Poems
Open House

*For Children:*

Party at the Zoo

*Selected Prose:*

On the Poet and His Craft
*edited by Ralph B. Mills, Jr.*

# STRAW FOR THE FIRE

# STRAW FOR THE FIRE

*From the Notebooks of*
*Theodore Roethke*
*1943–63*

---

SELECTED AND ARRANGED BY
DAVID WAGONER

1972
*Doubleday & Company, Inc.*
GARDEN CITY, NEW YORK

Grateful acknowledgment is made for the use of the following poems by Theodore Roethke: "A Nest of Light," *TriQuarterly*; "All the Semblance, All the Loss," *The Michigan Quarterly Review*; "The Root of the Wind," first published in *Mademoiselle*; "Straw for the Fire," "The Stony Garden," first published in *Poetry*, Copyright © 1964 by Modern Poetry Association; "In the Large Mind of Love," *The Hudson Review*, Copyright © 1966 by The Hudson Review, Inc.; "In the Lap of a Dream," *The Atlantic Monthly*; "The Proverbs of Purgatory," "I Teach Out of Love," *Shenandoah*; "The Loveless Provinces," *The Yale Review*; "The Things I Steal from Sleep," "The Dance of the One-Legged Man," *Poetry Northwest*, Copyright © 1968, 1970 by Poetry Northwest, respectively; "In the Bush of Her Bones," *The Southern Review*; "First Class," *The Antioch Review*, Copyright © 1969 by Antioch Review Incorporated; "The Beautiful Disorder," *Pebble*, Copyright © 1971 by Greg Kuzma; "Heart, You Have No House," *Voyages*, Copyright © 1971 by National Literary Magazine, Inc.; "Words for Young Writers," *Saturday Review*; "Father-Stem and Mother-Root," *Denver Quarterly*, Copyright © 1969 by The University of Denver; "The Wrath of Other Winds," *Malahat Review*; "The Dark Angel" and "The Poet's Business," Copyright © 1971 by The University of Oregon; "The Right to Say Maybe," *Seattle Magazine*, Copyright © 1969 by King Broadcasting Company.

Library of Congress Catalog Card Number 78–175404
Copyright © 1968, 1969, 1970, 1971, 1972 by Beatrice Roethke
All Rights Reserved
Printed in the United States of America
First Edition after a Limited Edition of 250 copies

# CONTENTS

Introduction                                                9

Straw for the Fire (1953–62)                               19

## Poetry

In the Lap of a Dream (1948–49)                            27

A Nest of Light (1948–49)                                  34

The Loveless Provinces (1948–49)                           38

All the Semblance, All the Loss (1948–49)                  43

The Stony Garden (1949–50)                                 49

The Wrath of Other Winds (1949–50)                         53

In the Bush of Her Bones (1949–50)                         57

The Dark Angel (1950–53)                                   60

Love Has Me Haunted (1950–53)                              63

The Dance of the One-Legged Man (1951–53)                  67

Father-Stem and Mother-Root (1951–53)                      71

The Root of the Wind (1951–53)                             75

Heart, You Have No House (1951–53)                         80

The Middle of a Roaring World (1954–58)                    83

I Sing Other Wonders (1954–58)                             91

Recall This Heaven's Light (1954–58)                       95

She Took My Eyes (1954–58)                                100

The Plain Speech of a Crow (1954–62)                      104

In the Large Mind of Love (1954–62)                       108

The Things I Steal from Sleep (1954–62)    113
Between the Soul and Flesh (1957)    118
The Mire's My Home (1959–63)    119
The Desolation (1959–63)    125
My Flesh Learned to Die (1959–63)    129
And Time Slows Down (1960–63)    132
The Thin Cries of the Spirit (1959–63)    135
My Instant of Forever (1959–63)    139

## Prose

All My Lights Go Dark (1943–47)    147
The Cat in the Classroom (1943–47)    160
The Turn of the Wheel (1943–47)    166
The Poet's Business (1943–47)    170
Words for Young Writers (1948–49)    180
The Proverbs of Purgatory (1948–49)    190
I Teach Out of Love (1949–53)    193
First Class (1950–53)    203
The Right to Say Maybe (1948–53)    213
The Hammer's Knowledge (1954–58)    224
From Roethke to Goethe (1954–58)    227
The Teaching of Poetry (1954–58)    231
These Exasperations (1954–58)    235
A Psychic Janitor (1959–63)    243
The Beautiful Disorder (1954–63)    252

# INTRODUCTION

At the time of his death in August, 1963, Theodore Roethke left behind 277 notebooks—most of them spiral notebooks—full of a miscellany of fragments of poetry, aphorisms, jokes, memos, journal entries, random phrases, bits of dialogue, literary and philosophical commentary, rough drafts of whole poems, quotations, etc., and 8306 loose sheets (as a rule, these represented a second stage in his method of composition: a movement from notebook to clipboard as he began to track a poem into its final multiple versions, after which he would move on to typed drafts, revising heavily). It is difficult to describe both the bulk and the character of this material: Roethke apparently let his mind rove freely, moment by moment in the early stages of composition, from the practical to the transcendental, from the lame and halting to the beautiful, from the comic to the terrible, from the literal to the surreal, seizing whatever he might from the language, but mulling over and taking soundings of every syllable. This prodigious output, not even counting the typed, reworked drafts or his voluminous teaching notes on other poets, now occupies twelve horizontal feet of library shelves in the University of Washington Manuscript Collection.

He wrote all of the material in this book between the years 1943 and 1963 inclusive. Prior to 1948 his note-taking was much less extensive, far more tightly controlled and purposeful, and consequently the fragments of poetry are less interesting. And prior to 1943 even his prose entries are tentative or perfunctory.

As datings in his own hand prove, he returned to completed notebooks, often after an interval of several years, and hunted for what he could use, recombining old and new images, lines, or whole passages on related themes; these fragments in their turn would apparently suggest new rhythms, associations, and ideas, out of which a new poem would usually evolve. To put it mathematically: roughly a third of a typical poem written by Roethke in, say, 1955 would consist of fragments extracted from notebooks two or more years old, occasionally from fragments far older.

The only ways I can account for Roethke's not having used the material in this book are, with the poetry, 1) he was sometimes dealing with material too painful to complete; 2) he would allow himself freedoms which in cold retrospect seemed too loose, though years later he might rediscover exactly such a "new" workable style; 3) he was unable to feel through to its imaginative conclusion some difficult idea; 4) he loved incompleteness, perhaps because it represented a promise that he would never exhaust himself (see the epigraph for this book); and, with the prose, I need only cite his deep suspicions of himself as a lecturer and essayist to account for his reluctance to draw his ideas into more manageable forms.

I can't presume to call the forty-two pieces in this book poems or essays. As far as I know, literary glossaries have no precise words for what has happened here, just as literary history probably has no clear precedent for the problem Roethke left behind. I know of no other major poet who has passed along so much unpublished yet publishable work (with the exception, of course, of those who scarcely published at all in their lifetimes); and he compounded the problem by leaving most of it in his favorite forms of disorganization. I felt when

I undertook this job that if I didn't arrange these fragments thematically, using something like Roethke's own methods as I had come to know them in public and private between 1947, when I was his student, and 1963, by which time I had been his friend and colleague for ten years, they might remain unread and unknown for many years, except perhaps for extremely diligent scholars. I think of this as my primary excuse, my primary justification, for taking what may appear to be liberties with the work of a great poet.

To describe as exactly as I can the nature of these "liberties": all the words are Roethke's; I have added nothing; asterisks mark off the individual fragments as they appear in manuscript; an ellipsis (a mark Roethke almost never used in his own writing) indicates the omission of 1) an alternate line when the poet sketched out two or more versions without deleting all but one, 2) a dwindling of the impulse that produced the passage (i.e., an incomplete or illegible phrase), 3) an intervention of the irrelevant (i.e., a sentence or two of an introduction he was supposed to be working on instead of a poem).

The fragments are arranged dramatically, not necessarily chronologically. Roethke himself set me the example by seldom composing chronologically, by writing poems inside out and/or backwards, frequently across spans of time similar to those indicated at the head of each individual piece. Therefore, one passage marked off by asterisks may have been written in 1959, and the passage immediately following it in my arrangement may have been written the next or previous week or in 1962 or '63. The associations, then, or the unspoken transitions are mine, but they are carefully considered imitations of Roethke's own arrangements.

For instance, the prose piece I have titled "All My Lights Go Dark," made up of fragments from between 1943 and 1947, follows the patterns of his own self-induced breaks from reality (which during that period he hesitated to call drives toward God) by moving from observation, with the promise of revelation; to meditation and a sense of his boundless possibilities; to memories of childhood, what he called "the central mystery of life," and a sense of its loss; to fear and despair in which meditation turns to "mindless brooding"; to desperation (mislabeled boredom) and a subsequent flight into sober reality; to self-generated (perhaps auto-erotic) euphoria alternating with exhaustion and undirected sadness; and thence to the pit.

And as a later contrasting instance, the fragmentary "poem" I have called "My Instant of Forever," made of passages from the last years, 1959–63, derives its organization from the examples Roethke set in "North American Sequence" and in "Sequence, Sometimes Metaphysical": from an invocation, in fear, of the fearful God; to an immediate, seemingly effortless metamorphosis into the relatively benevolent subhuman; to the sense of simultaneously rejecting and being rejected by that role; to a breakthrough into a completely different dimension of the self, an at-oneness, an atonement before the "small light" of the soul, about which he once found himself so glib; to a discovery of his "deeper life," his particle of God.

If anyone objects to this process of arrangement as an invention of associations on my part, all he need do is consider each fragment between asterisks separately, taking his own risks (with or without asters). He may then easily pretend the organization of this book, aside from dates, does not exist. I would welcome any and all efforts of that kind, because anyone who did so would create, on his own, in the long run, in the place where poems are made, a better order out of these passages than I've managed. Or than Roethke cared to or had time to manage.

Early in 1964, when I first approached Mrs. Roethke with the idea of making something coherent and publishable out of the notebook material, she let me choose twelve notebooks at random (subsequently their dates proved to range from 1953 to 1962). Out of these, I made the first four pieces: "Straw for the Fire," "The Plain Speech of a Crow," "In the Large Mind of Love," and "The Things I Steal from Sleep." I have left these, hesitantly, perhaps lazily, but gladly, in very nearly their original forms, even though the time-spans are larger than those of any other selections. I like to think the title piece combines prose and poetry and shifts of mood in a way that Roethke's own conversation did, complete with associational leaps.

Thirty-nine of the forty-two titles come from phrases within the pieces they name; the other three—"First Class," a balance of Roethke's own memorable prose diatribe "Last Class," "The Proverbs of Purgatory," an allusion to one of his favorite works, Blake's "Proverbs of Hell" from *The Marriage of Heaven and Hell*, whose dicta he frequently quoted and appeared to live by; and "Words for Young Writers," a workaday title unassuming enough, I hope, to need no excuse—these are the only words of my own in the book.

Fortunately Roethke was scrupulous in his use of quotation marks (the notebooks are frequently interspersed with poems by others, copied in longhand, and notes from his reading), probably to avoid confusing himself when he would come back to "check" (his word) what he had written. At times, either for special emphasis or to reassure his later dubious self, he would sign or initial a passage of his own. These facts (and my own additional researches) lead me to hope I have included nothing which is not Roethke's own. Occasionally some readers may notice a phrase which he used somewhere in his *Collected Poems* or in *On the Poet and His Craft*. I have left them as and where they are because of their sometimes illuminating new (actually old) contexts.

Those who know Roethke's work will probably find no new themes here, but many new variations on his constantly recurring subject matter: love-hate for the full range of am-

biguous womanhood; records of his thrashing metamorphoses as
he attempted to become something other than his usually de-
spised self; nostalgic evocations of the greenhouse Eden; the
flabbergasted ecstasy of a man who has glimpsed the mystic's
Oneness, knows it for truth, but fears he may never have
it; his wars on God, beginning and sometimes ending in the
pit; the death-haunted man embracing his own death.

If the notebooks show nothing else, their extensiveness and
their intensity show the most wholehearted, energetic, even
uncanny devotion to poetry I have ever known of, an apparently
almost total commitment of time and attention. I hope the
forty-two pieces that follow may give some further evidence
that Theodore Roethke was one of the truly phenomenal
creative sources in American poetry.

*To the memory of*
*Theodore Roethke*

"The desire to leave many poems in a state of
partial completeness;
to write nothing but fragments."
—*from a note, ca. 1945*

# STRAW FOR THE FIRE

## (1953–62)

What dies before me is myself alone:
What lives again? Only a man of straw—
Yet straw can feed a fire to melt down stone.

❋

To love objects is to love life.
The pure shaft of a single granary on the prairie,
The small pool of rain in the plank of a railway siding . . .

❋

Am I too old to write in paragraphs?

❋

I need to become learned in the literature of exasperation.
      In my worst state, once I think of my contemporaries,
     I'm immediately revived.

❋

I always wonder, when I'm on the podium, why I am there:
      I really belong in some dingy poolhall under the table.

❋

O Mother Mary, and what do I mean,
That poet's fallen into the latrine,—
And no amount of grace or art
Can change what happens after that.

✣

And what is to be learned from the defilement of the body?
The devil knows a good deal.
From you, devious darling, one can learn the immense gaiety
of a seat-warmer.

✣

I don't know a thing except what I try to do.

✣

My courage kisses the ground.

✣

Sure I'm crazy
But it ain't easy.

✣

For each act of my life there seems to be a necessary purgatorial period: even the simpler things, like going to the store. What a bourgeois I am.

✣

Who hesitates is Fortune's also-ran.
He never leaves who teeters on the sill.
Once I was one; I can be one no more.

✣

I seek first and last, that *essential* vulgarity I once thought charming.

✣

Feeling's a hard
Thing to do well—
And slightly absurd;
I'd rather smell.

❋

Of all pontificators, those who prate of poetry are among
the most tiresome . . . including those aging Sapphos
who speak as if they had invented integrity.

❋

If you can't think, at least sing.

❋

In the very real and final sense, don't *know* anything. That
is what saves me—from you, dear class, and from
ultimate madness.
In every man there is a little woman.
A teacher needs his students to stay human.
Suppose you master one cliché—
You're a step beyond the horse: a horse's A.

❋

Anything that's longer than it is wide is a male sexual symbol,
say the Freudians.

❋

O ye apostles of refinement.
They wander, empty in their skin,
And see themselves but now & then,
And cannot tell you why or how
They got the wrinkles on the brow.

❋

I'm so poor I can't subscribe to my own downfall.

❋

A breath is but a breath
And the smallest of our ties
With the long eternities,
And some men lie like trees,
The last to go is the bark,
The weathered, the tough outside.

✣

I'd like to be sure of something—even if it's just going to sleep.

✣

God's the denial of denials,
Meister Eckhart said.
I like to forget denials
In bed.

✣

I feel like a pig; but there are worse ways to feel.

✣

Who adhere to the central
Can yet be subtle.

✣

One the keeper, one the guide,
One that merely stays outside;
One the one that will not stir,
One the expert fathomer,
One the wheel and one the spoke,
One a vaster cosmic joke.

✣

For we need more barnyard poets, *echt Dichter* of *Dreck und Schmutz*, poets who depart from the patio, the penthouse, the palladium.

✣

What words have good manners? None.

✣

Wake to my praise, you dead!
The old crow wheels and cries;
The cold night purifies
The rich life of the wood . . .

✤

Me, I don't want to die: I want to live to a long self-indulgent
    happy productive dumb old age.

✤

I sang a most uproarious song,
A tune a dog could understand,
Digging in this prodigious garden
For a long-lost bone . . .

✤

I was betrayed by my own hardihood.

✤

All bushes can't be bears.

✤

A cloud climbs to the moon:
Thought within thought can be
Bleak stone upon bleak stone.

✤

My face is running away.

✤

By light, light; by love, love; by this, this.

# POETRY

# IN THE LAP OF A DREAM

## (1948-49)

I often laughed in the middle of the night.

✻

My bones whisper to my blood; my sleep deceives me.
This motion is larger than air; wider than water;
Fly, fly, spirit. A strange shape nestles in my nerves.
Whisper back to me, wit. I'm ready to be alive . . .

✻

Stay with me, breath, while I cross the trestle.
Don't go away while I sleep . . .
I feel the eaters watching . . . from across the lake.
The curtain's no good. They see me even from behind the webs.
You ape's tail, it's your crossing time,
You can't always have a flat path.
Wing-dippers, they're brushing the bush of smells,
Whoo-ha, it's Old Harry, he's begun sewing my ears.
Once he held me over a tub of water.
Lap, lap the wind, and the pond wrinkled.
Is that a bird in the chimney?
I can hear a flower breathing.
There's a dead leaf scraping around the lilacs . . .
Again, that play of wings, a slow brushing.
Nobody believes me:
They're coming over the stones . . .
    I lay all alone
      In the lap of a dream,
      Far from the waters

That were my home.
Rocks began flowing
Down my valley,
The ground cried out
My secret name.
Alas, alas, that skin-soft courage . . .
But why, then, all these backward jumps, the mooring by
    dead water?
I had waves and singing birds even on the bottom bough.
Even the stinks talked.
Shapes would sing and withdraw, purest at evening,
In the last after-light when I lived close . . .
When leaves were alive, I clung tight to the side of a stone.
It never left me, the wall of blossoms.
My nose was never afraid. I blubbed with the eyes of a
    turtle . . .
How certain the light has become,
The dust has walked out of my house.
How I love this wood, the summery shafts of tomorrow . . .
The waters are breaking with light.
I hear him high in the tree.
The sun, the sun is coming.

*

Dear God, I want it all: the depths and the heights.

*

You can't walk away from your own shadow;
I have observed the quiet around the opening flower,
The numinous ring surrounding the bud-sheaths . . .
The point is, dear father, if I don't stop soon,
I'm going to become a sun-tanned idiot boy . . .
I have basted the meat and eaten the bones;
I've kept grandpa from crying into his beard;
All I ask is a way out of slop;
Loose me into grace, papa,

I'm up to here and I can't stop.
I can't scratch anymore. My lips need more than a snifter.
Give me the pure mouth of a worm;
I'll feed on leaves; I'm a knob waiting for the opening squeak.
Why must I wait here, sitting on my hat?
Who else caught the burning bush?
I'm blistered from insights.
Several times I've heard the slow sigh of what is,
The moaning under the stones,
And the flames flashing off wings, burning but not consuming.
But then, what happened? I lapsed back into that same terrible
            calm,
No more than a nose in a grave, the pits of an ugly dream.

✻

Deliver me from myself: my journeys are all the same, father.
Ends, ends, pursue me.

✻

It's a day for a wild dog. Don't speak of it.
This light leaves me behind.

✻

Semblance, Semblance, I'm cursed by the half-perceived.
Something has thickened my sight:
A scared dog cowering in a dream.

✻

Let instinct caper its crooked mile.

✻

I'm just a slavering dog among these lambs:
A man immensely dead, a pair of paws.

✻

My bones, beware. This flesh is settling down
And squeezes what I have . . .

✤

I rasp like a sick dog; I can't find my life.

✤

Through a web of a dream
My toes are alone, soft in the bog.
Nothing, touch nothing. This is the rat's change.

✤

I'm lost in my name.

✤

I must be more than what I see. O Jesus,
Save this roaring boy riding the Devil's blast.

✤

My hair grows an inch—I too am a world.

✤

An intense terrifying man: eating himself up with rage.

✤

Such a one as never milked a mother.

✤

You had the answers, eaglet,
Before you left the principality of tears
And stinks: already scruffed with lice,
Knowing the basest life of sticks, the slops
Of air flung by what grassy rains came there.
I met a man, a ruddy deceiver. He went behind
The wind. Pilaster's me shadow, you known ghost:
Galumphing toward me; a blonde and booted jack,
Half-hair, half-horn. I live and I suppose
An angel's offering. Space dropped me with a sigh:
Egg-headed, bald, a roaring bright behind,
Between a periwinkle and a crass baboon . . .

*

It's ha, it's hay,
It's jig-jig and jay,
And what do you do with the hind-most?

*

I practice at walking the void.

*

Ah, the jounce of his juice, a roundy bouncer
He was, sleeping, even alone, into more than himself.

*

A rampant triumphant fleshly mysticism . . .
Einstein, we're going up . . .
All prior negatives call. The ill partake of this nature,
The full spasm of human nature, not blankness and beauty.

*

It's all I can do, he said, to hold onto life.

*

The upward turnings of the leaves,
The firs, those heaven-stretchers . . .
My world's a pillow that retains my smell:
Hell's neither cold nor hot for the unwell:
The fields extend themselves to please the eye;
I can forgo their bleak felicity;
I would and I would not; all changes greet me . . .

*

He acquired, painfully, all the pleasures of a lunatic.

*

Such hops and leaps!
Sighs, sighs had no sequence, I lay among twigs
A blinking hulk, a fat man sick of himself,
Waiting behind the weeds . . .

*

The feeling: you are alone in the room. If you turn around you
     will not be there.

*

This hero has no horse: he's live and like
An uncle: look, he's groping for the sill,
Clutching at chairs. That's not enough
To keep him steady. La, la, the light falls.
I'm here alone . . . breathing like a seal.
A sleek nose snoring by a light.
My other self has gone away.
When the owls come I'll be there . . .

*

All your ideas, put together, make a well-appointed nightmare.

*

Inhabited by visions that
     Sweep out to the door,
He can scarcely hold his hat:
     The winds wipe up the floor.

Looks, once nature to the eye,
     Flee like startled mice;
All the things that he lived by
     He must value twice . . .

*

Death blossomed in his eyes . . .

*

Hurry, hysteric, we wake, those dreams forgotten:
The pool pellucid by which we sit.

*

The week-ends in ecstasy, father, I find slightly wearing.
In the end I always return to the same tanks and sheds of
    desolation,
The garbage cans are still there, and the walls with the ugly
    blood.
The mirrors are filmy. My neighbor wants to talk about human
    considerations . . .
I must grow thin, father. Give back my hair and I'll put straw
    in it . . .

*

The wind died with the light . . .
Sweet dear, I am away: this thinning tree
Reminds me of myself: who's left and daft,
We're all mad . . .

# A NEST OF LIGHT

## (1948–49)

Why shouldn't I sing to myself?

❋

For what we see is never purely seen,
Not final with its final radiance,
As if we were but animals a-gaze
In a gray field, and grayness all around,
A universe contained by walls of stone,
An ultimate of air, a final scene . . .
A sea-wind pausing in a summer tree,
A bird serene upon a nest of light . . .

❋

And shall we leap the trees as light as birds?

❋

I leap to the wind.

❋

A stretching time, a crossing time,
Taller than the longest sun-shaft . . .

❋

The day, the time, the light across that place
Where two things meet: a spider swings himself . . .

❋

Early early
That simple time
When eyes knew
The shine of seals;

Ditches at noon
Swarmed with stars;
The hills hummed;
The moon came out
Bright on the shells
Wet from the water
Of slacking waves.
O how could early
Otherwise be?

The summer haze
Stayed into evening;
The moon falling
Through the screen,
Making a cross,
Repeating a shadow,
The weedy fields
Sweet as freshets,
The nightwind blowing,
The blossoms dropping . . .
Light couldn't sleep;
It stayed all night,
Rocking with blossoms
With warm hands . . .

✣

There the air's early:
Back, back, to those dreams of falling,
To say things fond, hear singing,
The mould flushed with light,
Sun on the eaves, on leaves, on lips,
Sun glimmering on the strands,
Flush on the shiny stones . . .

✣

My longing separates like snow.

✻

Spinning down from the moon . . .
Phoebe of the far wood, how you pierce me with your cries,
Single and true, brooding in the tree's center . . .

✻

The moon's cool blood came down . . .

✻

My head flew away like a spark . . .

✻

On some slow-sliding moon-forgotten wave
I crept from a cry.

✻

I feel the weight of stars . . .

✻

A light-foot fragment sing
To bring us to delight.
We'll sing away the night,
Birds without wing, we pause
Beneath fruit-heavy boughs . . .

✻

Growing both ways at once,
Alive in the light, in the dark . . .

✻

Too much of me stays here. Am I still half asleep
From this early dream?
                        The bird circles; the swale darkens.
                        Something stirs. It is not morning.
I see what pierced me; and am impaled.
Yea, that shaft of singleness has me.
I have undone myself loving the shine on stones.
Must I forget the mice in the ferns? Yes.

It's still enough here among the webs and skeins.
That early dream recedes and then returns.
Is the first eye dying?

❋

The wind won't lift me.

❋

The veils and skeins, the horns, the heart of life, the sweet
    imperishable forms.

❋

The rising waters surround me. There's no falling star.
Here's the last place of light . . .

❋

And torment takes me further into joy . . .
The great wind's part of me: I see before
I stretch to this intention like a seed . . .
I have sunk down to rise. I see the stream
That bears me . . .

# THE LOVELESS PROVINCES

## (1948-49)

I cursed my being visible.

✳

What eats us here? Is this infinity too close,
These mountains and these clouds? On clearing days
We act like something else; a race arrived
From caves . . .
Bearlike, come stumbling into the sun, avoid that shade
Still lingering in patches, spotting the green ground.

✳

Summer stopped on the hill: the weeds came round;
Small breathers and sweaters, sly delicate algae . . .

✳

Fish-mouths nudging against walls.
Moths hanging on harsh light.

✳

Stared at the rock's vein, the light
In the round of my hand balanced a stone;
Among the ringed ponds, the warped sills, sun-blistered walls.

✳

Fat is no delicate dance. I'm tired of soft cadences,
The sly twisted answers to the asking spirit;
Give me at least the harsh light, the serene imbelic gaze
Of my groping animal fathers.

It's true enough I come from an ape, and at least twice a day
    return,
Chasing my tail, dizzy with intuition . . .

\*

All day, all day the wind whirled me out of myself.
I saw the sea rolling there in the field . . .

\*

The close and far seeds scattered like sand,
I saw my heart in the seed, in the harsh
Pits of that grainy loam cast back . . .
Those leaves, the chains of my being,
Lift along, light wind,
Ruffling the close fur of the field mouse . . .

\*

O blooms! O dew-wet trellis! O loops of blossom,
The seedskins that I fondled as a child . . .
The hillside's tremor at a root's turning . . .
Breathing, breathing lighter than nereids,
Shape out of the leaves, summer caller,
My looks had a voice: I came close
When I talked to the seeds . . .
They were mine, and I loved their disorder
As they rose with their secrets . . .

\*

Among rocks he'd be happy:
Longing for the pure state:
Midnight: and clucking birds,
A light shell sliding over water.

\*

Birds beating in the blood . . .

✳

I beg for air: another way to grace,
The dips and swoops, the journeys of a seed . . .
I sift, loose as the dust; I wind and wish.

Cold all the tongues, the brushings of sleek wings,
The fanning play of feathers, hands, and mice,
The least mysterious noises of the dark,
The sides of lifted leaves, the veering bats . . .

✳

Wind woke my hair; a tune died on a stone.
The dark heart of some most ancient thing . . .

✳

A branch like a great wishbone hanging on a wire.

✳

Who ate the rats? The rent was in the window.
I was tied to a bleak eye; a young sprout without a stalk,
The leaves slightly damp, an infant's neckcurls,
I was a flier at twilight, a young owl dipping down from a
          barn-loft,
All the shadows were thin. The backs of turtles glistened;
Who? How I knew the spoons before care caressed me,
A mouth of many touchings, better on the bottom,
I could talk to a log, a heap of damp under a tree,
Knowing a bird's proportion,
On jumping logs I could love like the goats,
A gloating bug with a skin like water,
Gibber-jab, my watery wits talked back to the many tongues of a
          long truth.
I rebelled against plates, clucking soft as a young hen,
And the sun fell on my feet, my pink toes agreed.
The beasts roamed my blood . . .
By noon I was delta-calm; asleep in my gruel,
Turning and sucking, all the angels flying.

My fingers waited for my feet . . .
Click-click went the shoes. A bush of a beard looked down.
My food came on a cracked plate.
My head went into my neck. The corners pointed . . .

✢

All dark is there. The mouth that cannot speak:
The tongue wound all around a mother-root.

✢

Dwell in myself, said the dark fishes.
I kissed the hand that hit me . . .

✢

Hoo-ha, he's here. A dead fly in the webs of a dream.

✢

Mice-ears, here's the grutching ghost.

✢

The true point of the spirit sways,
Not like a ghostly swan,
But as a vine, a tendril,
Groping toward a patch of light . . .

✢

I made a last kiss to the stars, a slow
Touch of love to somewhere else.
Among the up-sprung weeds I hurt my hands . . .

✢

A hug of something else
Walks in a dress of bones . . .

✢

He died wanting a god.
Yet God he was who by unloving care
Taught me to see things as they really were:
The loveless provinces of squeal and stink,

The sweat and smacks, the life of hoe and spade.
His unmysterious touchings served the roots
And blossoms well . . .

*

Sweet skin, farewell;
This widest house is his . . .

*

From this day count all time: I left him there,
Singing across that great abyss between us,
Goodbye . . .

# ALL THE SEMBLANCE, ALL THE LOSS

(1948–49)

Lack-love, sing some sweetness into your bones.

✳

Love, honor, and dismay,
So dear, so darling she . . .

✳

I fell on a beautiful thorn: a blunder of love:
Make me separate, mother of my bones,
My mouth cannot endure.

✳

Though the seeking heart shall find
   Nothing else to tell,
There are agents to forego
   All the semblance, all the loss,
   That the eyelids show.

✳

Her flesh lay siege to my breath.

✳

I have recovered the impulse to say someone is lovely.

✳

How far outside you are! How removed.
How sweet in your little love. How careless
Of self: how undone already . . .

✻

Such a tenderness, such a contempt for women! As well chide
      lambs for lamb-ness.

✻

My dear, dear darling, already far away:
You bush of smells, come back.
Sun's on the tendrils. Can't you hear me, honey?
I'm limp and lax, turtle-inert.
How long is ever? Can't you bear with me?
My trotting ghost! I saw you, lecherous and black,
Crossing my sheets, altering the stale air . . .

✻

My God, can't this culture support a few cads?

✻

The wind plants more than I.

✻

To know and to love: the same thing.

✻

Her kisses ask me what I am.
I went between those blossoms like a ram.

✻

Another woman: a change of tears.

✻

A laxity of spirit, fatal to love . . .

✻

It would seem that some kinds of emotion are a disgrace.

✻

Who hears the second fire? There's still a life
Beyond this vision, ardent as it is;
When singleness has gone,

My tears no longer tease me out of shape;
I bleed for somebody else.
My feet remember where they have not gone.
The stones say why not. Don't kiss me early.
I walked on a log out over the river.
I talked back to the water . . .
Soft-slicker went her feet.
She came for apples.
I died all day.

✤

I don't dare to be happy.

✤

Our two worst natures met that day and kissed
As knots of gristle in a glowing meat
That found themselves afire, spinning the spit
Until the deepest marrow steamed and hissed.

When we were done, no cook would look at us;
Shrivelled and twisted to a paltry shape,
Less than we were, dripping with oil and grease,
All pleasure sweated out, a loveless lump.

✤

At forty he's a fool who thinks he can deliver love so long
        denied . . .

✤

Act your heart. There's nothing else.

✤

She was wearing the flesh God promised me . . .

✤

I have prayed long that she might leave her skin,
And, leaving, she would ask me in . . .

✤

You're in a cage, all her kisses said.

❋

This stall becomes a pit. I would be loose
With joy, a creature springing in the sun,
A bounding goat of grace; I'm left with lust:
My frayed ends falter . . .

❋

Ho, spludder-guts, I said. What's that she-hippo doing in the
        hot weeds?

❋

The will bespeaks the wishing. Shall we slip
Between the trees of lust into the great
And pleasant plain of our true natures,
Keeping a quick eye where our feet go?

❋

What is the white of Two? Or the left of Love?
These perches are for birds, I can't sleep here.
Ah, love, drift over where the will
Lies so inert. We keep what we believe.

❋

Love isn't the fever I thought. You tricksy
Twisters thinning your life away.
That's the trouble with blood: it always mixes . . .

❋

Still, sit still, you secret heart,
And, wit, remind me how I love a woman . . .

❋

I am undone by love, and lose the art my mother gave me.

❋

There's a secret I have but haven't lived, he said . . .
Spring, and the seeds of my own death
Sprouted too fast.

I longed for a body lighted with love.
Instead, like the half-dead, I hugged my few secrets,
The hard-won bits of spiritual knowledge . . .

✻

When distance sleeps, then we shall meet to kiss:
Oh what an angel whetted that sweet tongue!

✻

All I learned is what I love.

✻

It's running now, drunk, sober and scared,
The flavor of my bones. These inches ask:
Why not, O you. So quick with change,
Why not persist in living? Love a tree,
Uncertain movement in the eye. Surprise
The day that you were born. O love, don't leave . . .

✻

He's one of those who kisses himself goodbye.

✻

All on a day, a day, a day,
Her light sweet flesh shall fall:
Her bright original wish
To sting me into being . . .

✻

Discussion leaves her body: words alone
Sustain her memory and only mine
Remember. They smite the wavy weeds,
Wakened by wind, all nodding to themselves.
I saw a number running in the sun.
Perhaps her pulse still lisps
One syllable of summer. She never knew
A ferny day. Dear love, the leaves are piled
Already on your sleeping name . . .

\*

In a deep deep yes. In all. I'm here alone and left.

\*

The world is where we fling it.
Lift me, long dream.
I'm leaving where I am for other loves
Than what I see.

# THE STONY GARDEN

(1949–50)

The stony garden of the spirit grows
Things never harvested in ordered rows.

❉

Time had no home in me.

❉

Sometimes when the leaves in the elm gather the last of light,
The eternal seems to come near me:
The evening wind ruffles the smallest puddles.
A stranger without a shadow moves in the old garden.

❉

Bring me, long ghost, another chance of light:
I'm waiting for the winter up my sleeve.

❉

The dried stalks, the shrunken
Ends of stems,
Once lively and light
In the white air,
In the far field where
The goldfinches swung,
Perched sideways
When the buds came out,
Pink and naked as young mice . . .

❉

How else? O it's all heeded: I'm strung-up on strings, a mangy
          chrysanthemum   head,   scraggly,   hunting   the
          sun . . .

✻

This earth gray with death—sweated and dead:
All pocked and pitted like cheap cement,
Broken to crusts; worm-riddled, blossomless—
Heaves here; only a stink of stalks. Hear
The cold scrapes of a hoe as we dig out
The corners of benches; empty these tables
Of humps and gourds . . .

✻

You whips of air:
I knew with what I staggered: I was crazed
Into a meaning more profound than what my fathers heard,
Those listening bearded men
Who cut the ground with hoes; and made with hands
An order out of muck and sand. Those Prussian men
Who hated uniforms.

✻

Deep in their roots, all flowers keep the light.

✻

What love-stirs! What loops and ropes of blossom!
Seed-skins kissed by the sun! The faint horns uncurling!
Bugs skimming through the oblique sunshafts!
And a song! Two songs, one outward, one inward
Echoing on each side of the glass,
One balanced on the edge of a wind-vent;
Another within, each singing things of the spirit,
This breathing, all upward, from leaves shining, wet,
The men wheeling in new dirt, their wheelbarrows creaking,
The sweat flashing on their faces, their palms wet,
Their palm-sweat flashing gold:
The day bright with its whiteness,
Those seeds in the next house already humping up dirt,

Heavy and hot. The bushels whisking past, that flip-flap fa-
    miliar,—
I was more than child when I saw this,
And time was immediate.
Something more asks me now:
See deeper than this:
That was a bright dancing of shapes
Before the pits, the sour lakes of the self,
Those times when alone I spoke to the wall.
New motions began in me, there in the filth,
But I came back, still with my blood.
All myself, too happy to ask
Why I was not struck down: haunting the shade,
I held my heart.

                    *

So the soul longs for its home. The things of earth
Fly from us in the lightest wind. Do we
Dissolve, you deepest delvers of the skin? How
Chaste the nakedness when nature faces us:
A cold particular bulk of porous bone.

                    *

In all those bones a love was crying out.
I never heard it then; I hear them now,
The words I never gave to a dying man . . .

                    *

How far's my father now?
Where has he gone, soft ears?
Tell me now. How far?
The sheep can't shear themselves.
Alone, alone, my cold ghost says.

                    *

Waking over, I went with the wind,
Praying with water:

My heels had been sleeping:
The brushing leaves kissed past my ears . . .
Sway, flowers, leaning like reeds in a wave,
More motionable than insects.
The morning-glitter!
Caressive green waves, under foamings of color,
The cold shall not touch you . . .

*

Shaken loose, like milkweed on the wind,
Sure of its crevice,
Or the root of a blackened stem, still linked with life.

*

Still air, still; almost noon.
The leaves dry on the trellis.
Will the green slime take fire, the slime on the benches?
This soil is past itself, half-gray, half-green . . .
The harp of the self stills.
Blue air, breathe on these nerves
Heat from the roses.
My hands are among blossoms,
Motion has narrowed,
My fingers natural.
Holding these, what do I hold?
More than a mold's kiss
Lifted into starlight,
Brought to this morning-shape.
My self breathes in these:
Star-flower, portal into the night,
Breathing brighter than water,
The twilight cannot whelm you.

# THE WRATH OF OTHER WINDS

(1949–50)

This wind presses me down like the straw of a broom,
Harsh to my face with its sand and flying sticks,
Flings me back against trees,
A wind lessening, the chimes of the spirit striking,
The lake still rolling, heaving, the trees, stiff,
Still bent eastward.

✣

Came to a coast at last: those final rocks, heaved up.
The shore of ghostly sticks: silvered like ancient hair—
The heart of trees rubbed down by salt and air
And tossing waves . . .

✣

What is the scud, says the wave
Breaking past the storm-walk. Some agitation
Greater than any motion of water; listen for the children,
Listen for human screams in the wind; as if
The center of fury has woken.
The young trees shake to their roots; the window's racketing
Wakens the youngest child: who hears in this howling
Cries of the dead . . .

✣

They said the swaying ceased: but now
That motion's greater. I feel what the great sea's for
Beneath its ancient mossy trees; my feet
Break on these roots . . .

*

Not ghastly but ghostly,
Mother of us all; made all of light,
At the end of the breakwater,
Under the sunken stones,
Beneath the planks, deep in an old ooze,
I shall find you:
Among the owls, far in the trees,
Beyond the coldest rushes
Where the lily has its daughters,
Great bird in the leaf-crowded dark,
Your wings deepen the dusk.
By the side of streams, where runnels brighten the hill,
Where the dark comes early, in late November,
In a dark place I saw another shape . . .

*

The bulks cannot hide us. These shades
Speak our especial desolation: the warped wind-beaten boards
Creak with our sighs, and changes come
Slowly as in the black approaching waves.
I sigh for a stair in this water:
And now, falling back, the sucking ebb-tide
Leaves the broken life of kelp and stones.
Yet I have the wind. I sing to the sand
A croon mother-remembered.
Wish and wake me, waves,
I've stood here for the last time.

*

How far a sigh comes.
Will the eyes stretch farther?
A light wind stirs in the pine needles.
In a long walk I lost the strands of dream.
Where is she, made all of light,

Oh the small shape, the dirt's cousin.
Send me a sign, for my spirit grows,
Awake and alive.

Should I forage the stones like a bird
Picking for seeds? . . .

Kinsman of air, I love you in this dark,
This time for nervous shapes:
Let something loose,
I face both ways at once;
A dreaming witness,
My fingers lax,
This mouth agape at clods,
A stranger to myself.

Haze is obscene, cold watery calm, go die within that womb.
These eyes are lakes of love in which perch play
And jump with bats.

The dark comes early here,
Tick-tick the seed that drops across my sill.
Close to the lips this mist: now all awakened,
I must walk alone and cold,
And deader than a ghost.
You're still bat-heavy, stooping over stones,
You're baited like a hook with light . . .

Who sighs? Ask yourself, prettybones,
The rings are from the pond, the river's fallen . . .

Now bend and touch the loam:
You touch what was and is.
Bone-deep in loam, you'll find what is,
All shadows start here, changeling,

Like the light, a full-air change.
So, tiring, fall into a kiss.
The mind wakes for its sleep, ready for dark;
And the wrath of other winds.

# IN THE BUSH OF HER BONES

## (1949–50)

She moved, gentle as a waking bird,
Deep from her sleep, dropping the light crumbs,
Almost silurian, into the lap of love . . .
She moved, so she moved, gentle as a waking bird,
The bird in the bush of her bones singing;
Woke, from a deep sleep, the moon on her toes.

✱

In the mixtures of her thought, a profound
Hiatus, dark on dark;
Between extremes I saw the vision catch
Light upon light . . .

✱

Words for the wind, I know:
She, dreamily lascivious, like a seed,
Just new to sun and water, swelled within
Until her deepest being had to heed
The strict compulsion troubling all her skin.

✱

To find that, like a fish,
What the fat leaves have—
How else, meadow-shape?
This fair parcel of summer's
Asleep in her skin,
A lark-sweet lover if ever there was.
To the north of a mouth I lie
Hearing a crass babble of birds:

The water is busy
In the place of beautiful stones;
The fountain
Hangs by its hair.

*

Dear witch, dear devious dove, I halfway know
The meaning of these giddy spirallings.

*

You haunt all my wakes and sleeps.
And what's between keeps time,
Or tries, to the blood of a bird.
A toad and a bear we'll be, moseying after lettuce:
Haunting the small paths, fish-slippery . . .

*

You sprouts that have! The air is airy.
My fingers can be hands, you king of the wrong ground,
Well of my ease. Which way?
I've sung myself back into sweetness.
The vines are all winding outward.
Once I was slow to shining.
But now my words are leafy, love.
I see! I see what sings.

*

You apt ready uncertain spirit,
I'm one with her wish:
Unwind, you spectral shapes:
If Eve has a way, I want to know.
That was a breeze I married,
And now I'm tilting at the weeds.
I basked in her breath . . .
It's a day to save.
And so out of her eyes I went sailing,
Like the first seed of summer on a long wind,

Twisting away, a small feathery shape
Sliding in the breeze of her breath,
No more of me left than a husk,
Less than a bit of cindery snow
Ticking over the stubble,
A slow feathery floater
Whisking by a child's ear.
Had I learned escaping down the wrong wind?
It was me in motion over the stones,
Over the dusty hedge.

✳

A flower all root she was,
Taking herself into the light leaf-mold,
Then lower into a grave
All her own.

✳

Use up the last light, love.

✳

Sweet stars, I'll ask a softer question: Moon
Attend me to the end. I'm here alone.

# THE DARK ANGEL

(1950–53)

In the dead middle of the sweating night,
I lost my name; and that was my delight;
I cried a name, I cried a name out loud;
I was the shape I was when I was born . . .

❖

What place could know him in that frantic hour
When he put off his being like a shirt?

❖

The mirrors melted down and flowed away,
And God had use of me on that dark day.

❖

In the womb, I refused death.

❖

No, not nothing, not unbeing's bleak stare,
The white walls of nowhere, the glassy ache
Of the raw desert, the alkaline Great Beyond.

❖

Nothing defined or final in itself,
All nights combined to make a blacker day,
The soul appalled by time's hyperbole.
Self, self, the stinking self offends my eyes;
My ears, my nose drop with my ancient knees.
I am undone by false propinquities:
Lipping a stone, and calling it a rose,
For hell is where I am . . .

❊

So desolate in this felicity,
So driven by extremes—Which way is Near?
I am a man becoming what I see . . .
And these loose flames become a single fire.

❊

Few of the blind are mad.

❊

John Clare, I know the way your spirit went:
Day after day, the lonely languishment,
Hours turn to minutes when true spirits laugh:
He loved the world, and cut his life in half.

❊

Christopher, help me love this loose thing.
I think of you now, kneeling in London muck,
Praying for grace to descend.

❊

Disorder, heraldic, magnificent:
Hate raging under the moon,
Ghosts bursting the rooms of a hurt heart,
While the winds lag
And all minds groan to recover
And kill the root of desolation.

❊

You lock of skin, pray keep this motion nice.
Why have I flung my reason that it sings
Without me, a country babbler by a sty?
My sympathy is sickness, so they say.

❊

The trees are breathing less. You, winky, sleep.
I've come to tear the sun out. Save me, mouse.
I'm done with every pretty thing.

✳

Those miseries took shape
And broke upon my path
As if the leaves took form
And scuttled into shade,
A shape of headless fur,
Brother to rat or worm.

✳

He'd lost the will to be. His various selves
Retreated, all, into the deeper grass,
Or pulsed behind a stone in the long field.
The green of things remembered the late rose
Shrivelled against the sill . . .

✳

Death's all: death's substance is this gray;
And the ground cannot save us. I'm a stone
Cast into ashes. See, the air's still! A fine fume
Drifts from one seed.

✳

The blood's appalling repetitions end.
One part of him was dying long before.

✳

To my dead self with its perpetual fear of death
I said Good-bye.

✳

Bow out, dark angel.

✳

You summer stallions, paw.
Grass widows, wives, weep well
For here's a noble lord of skin laid down;
This gap shall hold me.

# LOVE HAS ME HAUNTED

---

(1950–53)

Should I renounce my care, I would be kind,
Kind as a child; but fear is my close kin.
The slow moon hangs its beam; I shake my head,
Wishing and cursing;
Love has me haunted, hunted to this place;
Speak with the long eye, light.

❋

In that raw dark, in that black matted wood,
The final white, the mother-goddess stood.

❋

No wit of mine willed her near:
She came, light as an angel.

❋

At her approach, all emptiness dissolved.

❋

Cold was that heart; and every secret vein
Filled like old marble with translucent ice;
And yet I cherished her; and she was mine.

❋

Learned in motion, she
Made music with her bones
Until the trees bent down
With a wind-swept applause;
The bears sat on their paws
In wooded galleries.

Who stares too long
At stars may err
In thinking she
Is like a star
Burning the night
In slow delight.

✳

Eternity's the motion in my shoe,
She said, and cast her slipper off. And there,
A thin vein beat . . .

✳

Her round arm wound around my neck:
And I believed a lover's luck.

✳

Slow, slow, my willow-dear,
Her face framed in my arms.

✳

I want a flower's outwardness, she said.

✳

Her face recoils: she's narrowed at the eyes;
Unwilling prisoner of my intent,
What hound of spring would leave the lovely scent
Rising from ferny places?
I seek a country, not a continent
Cold cares away, the rivers of her thighs.
My nose believed her! O what ravishment.

✳

You're welcome to my ways, she said.

✳

Rasp and cackle, you shiny hags: here's the best way to be born.

✤

Growth's winter creep, the stretch of mouldy change,
The time's ripe for a roaring girl.

✤

My plenipotentiary of extraordinary invulnerable rubbish,
My button-eyed, goat-backed, meat-faced, slaver-lipped,
Prehensile, irrelevant virgin.

✤

Hurrahs for our halves, you schizoid minotaur. This virgin
bringing her own forest, a red joy with the eclipse of a kiss.
How sweet she speaks from this hyperborean calm, a dear
dove that does: I adore her motions on a lovely moony night;
may she be intelligently bridled by the eunuchs of disorder,
shaking out musty bustles.

✤

When we kiss we never see
Visions of futurity
Or the sharp stars reeling by:
There is only you and I,
Tracts of vastly laboring air
Whistling in some planet's ear . . .

✤

That moment came; that moment came again
And I looked forth upon the glittering sea:
In the bright noon I saw her gleaming skin
A mirror of my own mortality.

✤

By what so cold device have I been caught
In the loose strays of a less wanton wish,
I've paid for what I've had; and I am brought
Back to the muddy shore, a gaping fish,
The hulking carcass lolling by a lake,

Breaking small bale, and for another's sake.
No flenser needed to peel off this skin,
Loose as a colt's; and ruffled where she was.

*

She with her small cries speaks high in tweaky words,
With a lardy sweetness,
With her step light as a sandpiper's.
The breeze is black that kissed her shape away.

# THE DANCE OF THE ONE-LEGGED MAN

## (1951–53)

Sing all beginnings, sing,
Dance, dance, one-legged men:
We're not the same as then,
But worse in flesh and skin.
It's time that we begin . . .

\*

There's no place else: begin from where you are.

\*

As when a fish turn easily in low water,
Nudging out between stones,
Confused, for an instant, in some back-eddy,
Only to swirl himself forward,
Wetting a high stone with his flash of silver:
Himself and the water,
Himself his element.

\*

An evil more recurrent than the waves
Turns us to stone, or breaks us into halves.

\*

This veering—I'm afraid. I can't see myself clear
In any mirror now but shifting water. This is
How my mother went. Sometimes I'm several
And my choices snicker.

\*

I go out of all things only to be alone.
A bleak stone on a great flat shore.

❋

I have no native shape.

❋

I am by way of becoming
No more or less than I am.

❋

Uproot, pig. Uproot.
The coarse spectre changes. I'm loose
And alive to what I like.
That's where we all are.
Under the wind of this small change,
I find what I'm like,
Alive as a worm.
A knight of purest form,
I fly and pursue
The end we all love.

❋

Make me less clumsy, Lord. O make me light
Upon this ground; and make my shadow white.

This mottled shade betrays me as I am,
Shifting through choice, a player in the shade.

❋

In that coarse spasm of disgust there's not
An inkling of supernal thought;
And what I fear is fed by this delay,
This dragging down, this careless play
Before the stars; I brood on what
I cannot be . . .

❋

Detachment has no reference to the skin;
I'm really never here; I'm in
A daft superior daze . . .

✤

To take myself away from what I am
Is more than mortal being can devise:
I could be stranger to that common theme
Discovered in the mirror by my eyes:

We are bewitched by what we cannot see,
A poor self strung upon a foolish gaze,
A cretin's fancy is my highest praise,
I weep away my lips: I cannot be.

✤

I don't know what I am:
I'm in love with being born.

✤

This horny skin. I buckle with the waves
And roast in fire. Suppose a rock should sneeze
Me loose, unfasten me from earth before
My time and I went burning with the hay?
What breeds beyond my seat, or just above
My temples? These are sly matters waiting for a look
Behind the eye . . .

✤

Which of my winds will take
The downdrift of myself?
My help's not in me.
These ashes sift themselves.

✤

I've come to hate my own ecstasies: rich
Within me swims another thing: a whale,
Shapeless yet whole, and worse than Ahab had
Pursued: not white: a gray amorphous ghost
Of what we should not be.

*

Sit in the instant if you can
And you'll become another man:
And where you were will be a place
Still tenanted by empty space.

I lost my finger in a cup;
I could not bring the tankard up.
I pushed the wind before me as
I bumped into the man I was.

The sun's a burden for me now.
I cannot tell you why or how.
And that's the way it always is
With documented mysteries.

We look before and after, and,
Like Shelley, rarely understand.

*

Shine forth, you idiot forms,
With what I cannot see:
Essentiality
Of all ground-seeking worms.

*

Each thing's an end of something else:
I cannot hear a fainting pulse:
Farewell, loose metaphysic skin:
I would be out: you want me in . . .

*

What I am is no more!
I bid myself farewell.

# FATHER-STEM AND MOTHER-ROOT

## (1951–53)

For Father-Stem and Mother-Root—
The will sings to me now:
And all its notes are wild:
I'm quickened by a vow
To resurrect a child . . .

\*

I remember more than the far sun
Touching the vine, or the level light
Straight through the end panes . . .

\*

From those lost depths, a childhood without love, something
       may come anew, more real than it ever was.

\*

I was born under a heavy shade,
Loam-fire my father.

\*

The happy hats come at me.
I'm here but once.
I'm up, I'm up, you mother-melting flowers,
The dearest delver that ever was.

\*

My face washed in the milk of this morning.

\*

The weather's rich. I'll watch and sing around
The wind. I'm keeping close to home.

Thrum. Thrum. Who can be equal to care?
From all hands, something falls,
No burden of the wind. Outside, we're more
Than skin that circles in the light . . .

❉

Ho, ho, and it's all. I see in my sleep.
This stunned country of ourselves. What keeps
Our flesh?

❉

O gentlest light, descend
Far past the body of the moon.
Early to fire he was.
A ghost came to her lip; kissed once . . .
She took up with the wind,
I've never known her since.
As a rose, close-gathered,
Her eyes swayed me awake.
I need another needle.
The edges eat me.
     My love, my butter-melting mother.
You seem to be seized.
       By a dream.
All feathers find me, father.
I'm the frog's first love.

❉

We listen back with water to the seed:
Bend ears to being, making wind a wall,
Or lean above the blossom, as if the smell
Could wake our lazy ways . . .

❉

Now it's for the rain to take:
And runnel through
Where the worms went,

And the weeds will strike silver where
The chrysanthemum reared
Its waggish mane:
May all the late flesh dance
With whelms of how,
And sweet extremes of seed
Snore here.

❉

The flower heaves the stone.
Leave me to love
The last patience of looking close:
Which the child forgets.
In a low grapey place I remembered:
Only the desperate really survive.
The rest are dead, no more
Than ghosts on a thorn.

I wander where nobody lives. O lark so light,
Be keeping me by the streams.
The woods are ready to walk away.
Unwind, unwind, all shapes of life and death.
There's nothing here but shadows.

❉

I look from the stretches of dream.

❉

What's all? When's the sky night?
(I can't stop the questions).
Surely goodness and mercy
Dissolve me

Into another shade, revolving
Around my worst choice.
Now why is that?
I can't laugh:

Right or left
The news is wrong:
Wrung from a child's pain.
I would, but I can't

Kiss the world
As a child would,
Though my strong heart
Shakes up its bones,

I cry
For nothing less than what I truly am
As a being with brothers,
Dying.

# THE ROOT OF THE WIND

## (1951–53)

She walked with a cold grace, under the pure star,
With her feet arching over the white
Grass, a summery shape
Floating out and over
Where the thistles bent and dipped
With the wind's push
And the fields lay in wait,
Lay open with love for her . . .

Was that the wind woke me? she asked,
A daytime sleepwalker, sleek at the knees,
Her hair trailing behind,
A fleece needing a needle, pins, ribbons,
Something to make it walk with her.

Hear my tears wake with you, walking the windy
Ways where my father and mother went
Out of their hearts; life left
Us all out on that day
You played maiden-without-a-hat,
Light strider, the purposeful
Thighs breaking past
Wheat, oats, barley, a brazen
Hussy denying the heat . . .

✱

The buds fell open before me;
The grass white at the roots,

Ready with answers,
The skeins of green, the twisted
Lay at my feet: surely all
Particulars attended:
The clean lips of the snake,
And the flame-wrapped tree,
A sea-bird riding gently
A slow surf of light,
They turned with me . . .
And the ground alive
Lifted the ends of my bones:
I rode a dolphin of moss;
My heels kindled the loose leaves.

After this came the swift
Heaven of her look: yet the light
Never staled . . .

❋

In the rich valley of your gaze
I pause, as if in sleep,
A man half-tranced.

❋

For I have left my mind, and put on love.

❋

Give me, give me, wind.
Dissolve my curious ways . . .
Light as a bird in snow,
Light as the wind
Winding around a tree,
A sapling shivering,
This small ghost moves.
She loves.
She likes it fine,
A winter-watery drowse,

A serpent's pause,
A time to climb.

✻

I've plucked the root of the wind! Her kiss gathers
The great surrounding air . . .

✻

For her great sigh could sheer a field:
One breath and all the stems are down:
The branches shaking far from there.

✻

A bird sang loud and let the moonlight in.

✻

The skin's my end, and that's my name.
In the cove of my care, the little fishes love;
Be quiet, Quick. Be happy, Hair.
Of flesh, be faster in this minute
Before the conscious dying,
My verb, my pillow,
My hay, my honey,
Her eyes go out in the close moon . . .

✻

What time to noon, dear creature? Shall we end
Our days by saving what we cannot spend?

✻

When she touched me I could not think a thing
Except the details of her ravishing . . .
Disorder and disunion come to terms:
Decrees are final when they're made with worms.

✻

My rising met the rising of her breath
And we were locked in the embrace of death.

❋

Her eyes swayed me awake.
But the wind kept me waiting.

That water-wish went away.
You scared only my body, she said.
The hedge was weeping its leaves
Down to the last seed . . .
Do you sing always in corners?
That's ever! that's ever! she said.

In a day for rocking and bobbing,
We went spinning down
Where the bushes were never bears,
And the shade moved along lanes . . .
How well our wishes went. The ugly and lovely
Rolled in our gaze.

Then, with a break in the sun,
All the juttiest ends talked at once:
The ripe side of love, and the bees' welcome.
The close grains danced in the dirt,
The cats gathered;
An angel with hips of stone
Nestled in my nerves;
The dark rolled;
I want another joy, she said,
Melting, a farther moon . . .
I'm afraid of what you do,
You fall of green going away . . .

Dear love, dear lady-in-a-tree,
Shade delicate as feathers.

Give pause, you fiends that keep our kisses back.
We're veering toward ourselves . . .

She's for the rain to take. A dream away.

# HEART, YOU HAVE NO HOUSE

(1951–53)

What wronged ghost raves in this house?
I cannot say. Time's dying on the moon.
I hear the minutes limping round and round.

✼

I moped all day with a wrong word.
How can I ever sing? What's right enough,
Clear in the dark, clouds up by day.

✼

Forgive me this minute; the hours are creaking
Past these midnight bones.

✼

He's here, the very father and son of death
Who shakes the dark with his look.

✼

My long fathers are calling.
I hear the cries from the muck and sand . . .

✼

In the deep dead of that night, I laughed for a love,
And I quickened that I should die.
By these deprivations of spirit and sense
By the moans I have never heard,
What heavenly candle flickers in my flesh
Faltering toward another shade?

*

Midnight's my measure. Who
Can tell me what avails
When false light fails?

*

I'm called by the light and the dark
To please my inches.
What comes will kill me.
That death is easy.
Woo me another way.
The gun is too pure.
My sweet's here.
Kiss this.

*

I'm sick of being well; but that is ill-
Ness. See, my lips are loose with meanings not
Intended: I lie down with my thought,
Careless of sleep.

*

One can go mad anywhere. O reason, are you there:
What's here and not beyond
Is what I'll have.

*

Believe the right bone.
Surface calm; disorder within:
Space ties me. Recede, coarse dream.
I can become the leaves, a twisty bird,
Rise from the true
Nest of this change.

Outside the frost sparkling
Along the edge of the chair,

Close to the cypress frames,
On the black wooden fences,
Along the rutted road-crown,
The dirt glittering
Brighter than fresh waves
Or moon-washed phosphorous.
                    Each time ever
                    Around a cloud,
                    Easy and early,
                    On top a thistle,
                    The horny rootlet
                    Hunting for water.
I've been to bed with a dream. The gods remain.
In the harsh short hand of subliminal depths I've spoken,
No sleek captain of intuition or tapir of redolently disordered
        mortal life . . .

✤

Such is my heart's own stuff. I can renew
Myself with images of broken trees,
The coarse delights of an unfaltering rage.

✤

Heart, you have no house.

# THE MIDDLE OF A ROARING WORLD

(1954–58)

I knew a fool for luck
Who never changed his ways
Until his own soul's lack
Disturbed his later days.

✳

I slept with Yes, but woke to No.

✳

The exhausting fight against the inner fatigue, the soul-sickness.

✳

Show me what rest I have, and I'll become restless.

✳

There's a part of me that doesn't care: maybe that's the part *I*
cherish.

✳

I ate the Lord, and choked.

✳

I ate myself to live, and woke a fiend.

✳

The familiar longing to be ill.

✳

My babbling's nearer; I will feed the moth.

✳

All by myself, it's no disgrace
If I fall flat upon my face,

Drinking the things I should not drink,
Thinking the things I should not think.

The shades are down, the fire is burning.
My fattened ego is returning,
Not on the wings of noble song
But dragging a slack shape along.

O who's that figure on the walk
Engaged in incoherent talk,
Dragging his bulk across the sill?
Its shape is scarcely visible.

❈

Dazed on the sill, myself I would escape;
Swaying in time, my flesh a heavy weight,
I lean to love, and yet I dare not leap.

❈

The sun's never down for excessive men;
Their bellies light themselves a fire;
Who dare to romp from dawn to dawn.

❈

The grandeurs of the crazy man alone,
Himself the middle of a roaring world.

❈

Be aware, thighbone, shin, callous above my shoe. I am more
than the sum of my parts.

❈

I can't be human. I haven't the time.

❈

Madness is closer than we know.
I'm at too many removes from what matters;
I climb into the face, not the heart, of my neighbors.

How to trammel this love that continues speechless?
I would nestle in many laps,
But I cannot shake off this ennervating sadness;
I retire before tedium, the decrees of mops and mirrors,
I've stopped being a bird; appearances consume me;
The breath of a child's hair no longer holds me . . .

❋

This deepening terror I myself have sought.
What's horror but a cave the mind has made
With chalking walls, and nothing hanging down,
No thread dropped from a spider, no bat dung,
But only weakened light the lengthening afternoon.

❋

To possess or be possessed by one's own identity?

❋

The self, the anti-self in dire embrace.

❋

Instead of embracing God, he hugs himself.

❋

I spent myself in mirrors, like a whore.

❋

The mirrors laughing with their dreadful eyes.

❋

My belly laughs because the mind
    Thinks nothing funny;
But through my veins and without end
    Pours a prodigious money.

❋

Clearly watched, stretched forever a chance in the
shade, all out of time, a fierce moan in the dark, holy God is
wearing the wind out.

The terror of existence: the staring of chairs and tables
in the close middle of his nerves, all life an echo of himself.
The heavy years have me.
I long for my own land, in this country of bright air.
I shall answer all letters.
A style, dry, impersonal, cold, hard—in other words,
classic.
And that secret of a blanching ghost . . .

✳

The wing-tip of madness for Baudelaire: me, I live in the aviary.

✳

I can become what I will,
He cried, and grew a tail.

✳

Can I become that philosophic man
Without the sanction of philosophy?
One thinks too long in terms of what to be—
That grandeur of the crazy man alone
Who thinks imagination is the Soul
And that its motion is perpetual.

✳

With many myselves I stole away,
Laden with leaves for money,
My hair full of sticks and ferns.

✳

Hunting for a house like an animal hunting for a hole.

✳

I seem to lose connection with what is:
I find I'm tethered to another moon . . .

✳

In euphoria: a terrible fear that I would not live long enough
to achieve the full essence of experience.

❧

In euphoria, little work. But perhaps the source?

❧

      I can't go on flying apart just for those who want the benefit of a few verbal kicks. My God, do you know what poems like that *cost*? They're not written vicariously: they come out of actual suffering, *real* madness.
      I've got to go beyond. That's all there is to it.
      Beyond what?
      The human, the human, you fool. Don't you see what I've done. I've come this far, and now I can't stop. It's too late, baby, it's too late.

❧

My own agonies, which I once thought comic, have become more terrible with the passing of time.

❧

Acting one's age is just a form.

❧

I not only burn my candle at both ends: I send off pyrotechnical displays from my behind.

❧

It's very hard work trying to be naughty for a whole community.

❧

When I go mad, I call my friends by phone:
I am afraid they might think they're alone.

❧

The mystical position is somewhere
On the left bank of the derriere.

❧

I want to be a mystic of the armpit, with a private region all to myself.

❋

Was it my time for writing poems about McCarthy or my time
for sending out fresh salmon or the time of playing happy
telephone or my time for dictating memoranda about what's
wrong with America? . . . or my time for crying.

❋

Dear Diary—I mean, Dear Dictaphone: When I face you, black
ear, I lose half my mouth. What a horror of holes I have:
could that mean something? Perhaps, I had best put up an
umbrella.

❋

The doctor came and punched me with sedation,
And objects swam back to more close relation;
But still my raging spirit would not tame;
And I took baths; I wallowed and I yelled
(Thank God the old St. Regis is well walled);
And yet each morning I was brisk and bright,
My necktie on, three pairs of pants on tight . . .

❋

Why's my hand, long wisdom? I see this shape's away.
We live by being what we should not be.

❋

I have made friends with the barometer.

❋

Instead of a devil with horns, a serpent with scales
(Beautiful would they be in this dark);
When the night-nurse wheezes her pieties,
I confess I would rather eat than pray:
A prisoner of smells, I stretch in two directions
And would laugh from a cradle of burning pitch;
It's no time for crying:

Beware the perilousness of a long life!
Nevertheless, I retain a certain suspicion of death
In its more minute forms.

❋

One view: I'm sick, therefore the world is a hospital.

❋

(To his psychiatrist): I really believe in fate: why else would
I have such a child as you for a spiritual counsellor?

❋

I was nicer nutty: I could make up my mind. I was generous.
I was aware of immediate reality; too aware, alas, with a sense
of danger like a sleepless animal or a pursued criminal. —What
am I doing, writing prose?

❋

I sought release from my unsteady blood,
A creature not myself, plagued by the moon,
My life-beat measured by uncertain tides;
Adrift in murky waters, while the gulls
Screamed overhead.

❋

How imperfectly dead we all are! Should not the spirit take
over? My flesh needs a new place.

❋

Is the flesh less, after all the importuning?
We pay for the spirit's daring.
The soul stands, lonely in its choice,
Waiting, itself a slow thing,
In the changing body.

❋

I have beheld you, other world, I swear.
The last wrath faltered, falling to a smile.
I'm bruised and soiled, a transitory man . . .

*

Who else can tell me what I dare to say?
All things prepare for the mysterious day
We live yet do not live, perpetually.

*

The sense of something ripped out of a deep consciousness: Be
still, great silence.

*

A man struggling to find his proper silence.

*

O my poor words, bear with me.

*

My name is numb.

# I SING OTHER WONDERS

## (1954–58)

I swear by all fountains
Of an old heart;
The true ease
Of summing up;
A wasp drinks
From my cold cup,
Delighting in sugar
Like a true bee . . .
I sing other wonders
Than my heart's slowness:
In the inner eye
A bird quivers,
Throbbing my heels
With a throat's shimmer.

❊

Lilt where I live, you long throats,
I haven't sighed for a year.

❊

Five songs away, a whistler by himself
Stayed to his branch, a working fellow too,
And gave against the wind his throaty throb.

❊

The summer balances upon the leaves
Its several lights.
I see the shadows in the shade, a sun
Deep in this green, the singing of the root.

✳

Granite on granite pressing the earth down,
Each singing thing straining to come to form,
Made one by light on dark, stark in the sun.

✳

In a country crying for gods the stones give tongue,
While the slashed logs lie still
In the fat shade, thick as moss,
The silver sides sliding with snails,
The sly birds close:
Come to me, towhee,
Close-hopper, pecker of seeds,
A face floats out of the sharp ferns,
All this shuttling in the sun,
Motion profound as song.
Come, come, you summer sounds, a leaf away,
Who billow up my sleeve like a small breeze,
How am I here?

✳

That question cries again—
What is the least we know?
I call the slug my kin,
And move with those born slow.

✳

Hermetic fellows who
Know what the soul can do,
Whose unsuspecting eyes
Make angels of house-flies.

✳

Under the whistling eaves, I heard the swallow
Flutter his wings against the midnight roarer,
The storm that came too close to my own pillow,
The lively devil leaping through my mirror
The flash of change.

*

I can project myself easier into a flower than a person.

*

    I change into vegetables. First a squash, then a turnip. Finally, embracing my sides, hugging myself in the delights of self-possession, still a virgin to all relevance, my leaves at once press and expand; I steam in the morning mist.

    I become a cabbage, ready for the cleaver, the close knives.

    I endure peculiar worms, green as my leaves, who curl in the choice parts of my interior, my once so-private world. But there is nothing I can do.

    She deserts me for a blonder vegetable. Since then I have been committed by my roots to a time and a place.

*

Getting loose: I took my place among the lashing eels.

*

And you, sweet dear, the mouse of joy,
Dance, dance, with the sad animals
And wear the shape the lions wear.

*

May I live on, in the bull's nose, in the drooping tail of a sheep, in the sharp slide of the come-down hail, a hero to ten stones, the calf's answer, smelling the halls with my hairy heels.

*

The dark went out of my several selves at the coming of day;
I thanked God for giving me language back,
For a time at least; and my random rages are over.
I've written my whispers down: and spare the good sheets none;
Still, deeply still, a creature of serenity, a spider climbing a
    trellis,
I flew out upon the world.

❋

The sea's where I never was,
So the sky's my home and its long billows,
A lake in flame I have known,
And the slow sounds
Over glassy water
Only broken by the skimming bugs,
The nameless wrigglers.

❋

These insects teach a man
To be anonymous.

❋

I'm by all waters now.

# RECALL THIS HEAVEN'S LIGHT

## (1954–58)

I'm set in one direction: toward the sun.

\*

First the far trees ablaze, and then the last end-panes,
The shafts of light settling like long planks being lowered into
    place
Until you felt you could walk out toward the sun
On its own light.

\*

Recall this heaven's light, you speechless man.

\*

A mother's lap
Coiled like a snail,
A dolphin's curl
Of downy bones.
The winds brought hair;
The two trees spoke,
Feathered a fish
The sun reared.

Beware! Beware!
The leafy one,
Whelped in the dark . . .

\*

I slept above those houses, in a windy porch between the
    elmtrees,

And how I loved water, even a puddle shined with the face of
    the lord.

*

How many places for those shy
Delights of the self; the arbors between
Long sheds where the useful tools
Rest from their labors; the lumber
Piled like bread in tiers, wagons
Ready to rumble away . . .

*

Greenhouse: this hell and heaven at once, this womb of
    cypress and double glass.

*

. . . And my father grew you in houses six hundred feet long,
    stems four and a half feet high
(Thirty-five dollars a dozen to select customers).
Once he lifted me up, only five,
To look at what he had created
With the liquid-manure machine and sixty-five men to help
    him,
To say nothing of God, THE FLORISTS' REVIEW, and the
    power of steam, sun and water,
They came out of a lovely tremendous stink, straight as bam-
    boo in the stem,
Close-budded, wrapped in their secrets, vestal virgins,
How he hated to cut them!
And the men went in, secretly, in the early morning,
To gather their supply for the stores, and the funeral orders . . .

*

That hunter's eye could see a flower's flaw;
It was the true invisible he saw
When the true shapes extended on the stem;
The shimmer of the rose extended him.

He knew the world and its ferocity:
Yet lived in love: he loved what he could see.

✳

As was that other, that impetuous one—
Believing both his eyes, the angel sloth,
The blest bright business of the summer bush,
Cutting great scallops in his father's cloth;
The river's roily boy, roaring at noon,
Plagued by my nature, and a sensual leap;
He learned to live by hanging on a lip,
And took my pleasure in a lively lap.
He twinged the night with rosy lion roars;
And yet a dog could smell him and his fears.
A stone-rocked boy, a skinny bitten child.

✳

### The Reproof

I took his censure—like a man?
No, like a child, a father's child.
The words blazed red across my face:
The more he struck, the more I smiled.

✳

My grief was excessive, but I recovered.
For death-into-life was the rhythm of the greenhouse,
The men emptying the parched benches in the hot days of
        August,
Piling the gray exhausted earth outside,
Wheeling the shrunken stems, the maimed roots to the ever-
        changing flower-dump—
Then the seed, the seed, finer than rose-dust,
Renewing the new loam, finely sieved, under the sloped glass,
And the knobs of growth breaking from the tips of fresh cut-
        tings,
In the flat boxes of sand, in the low side-benches,

The fuchsias, the swaying hydrangeas,
The callas, yellow at the tip, early in September,
The roses fading into wrinkled papery knobs.

❋

We are not young anymore; the glacial
Foot never passed here shyly; not even
The animals really cared for these marshes.

❋

The Siberian pitilessness, the essential ruthlessness of the
        Middle West as I knew it: as an accepted thing.

❋

My immediate, I'm in love with your last leaves,
Will feather out your swaying,
What's a tree? The light's child.
I'm father enough.

❋

When all slow feathers speak a secret noise,
And fields all sway beyond us, like the sea,
And morning sings the news; and roaring boys
Leap in the light of white eternity:
When cabbages and buds unloose their fire
Until the meadows blaze like lakes at noon.

❋

The trees are gone, all the white glass is gone,
The concrete benches bolster paving-stone.

Once I was young, and walked a flowery way;
A greenhouse is its own eternity.

❋

Form is a father: when I looked for form,
I found a leaf, and on the leaf a worm.

\*

Whose lips dare speak? I fear the cold Therefore
And pass, unfeeling, at a feeling's grave:
A child died here. I was that likely child.

\*

Now I must go beyond:
Who else knows where I am? I'm
A fish lurking close to a boat, a child holding the net,
I live through my black tears, a child of light.

# SHE TOOK MY EYES

### (1954–58)

Who'd change the motion in her thighs?
They give such pleasure to old eyes,
   I'd have her walk around
All day where ancients gather to
Exchange the news of me and you,
   And all whose limbs are sound.

John Suckling would delight in her:
She walks a path: there is a stir
   Most definite and profound.
Among the peaches and the pears
You'd swear their leaves had eyes and ears
   And whistled a low sound.

✻

She looked as if she had been basted lightly in butter.

✻

O sweet my dear she's lovely in her shoes;
She dances out the day.
Could she, love's all, remember what she was?

✻

But who found out the spirit's harmonies
Without enquiring what the spirit was.
She ravished more than ears; she took my eyes
Into her own, and made them glitter there,
And my close look turned to a bovine stare.

\*

I knew where danger lies: in my own lap;
The still fire at the stem, the burning crown . . .

\*

The fullness of that pulsing, self-protective, malodorous, car-
nivorous, lecherous fever.

\*

I've run from where I am.
Here's the long heart of an old love.
I'm ready for your wish.

\*

Some cannot tell or dare not say
What they do in the dark.
Her slow song sang the night away:
My true love loved her work.
The road I rode upon all day
Had but a single fork.

\*

No, No, go on, her spirit said.
We can out-climb the devil and the dead.
Storms rose and fell over her comely head.

\*

Men see their Beatrice with a luminous shimmer, a numinous
haze, a close and yet far quality: but what do women
see?

\*

The secret lies in women—who said that?
What woman ever thought she thought she thought?
O the grave dangers in a woman's brain,
Her being glitters with the pure inane.

❊

All this sensual play
Between you and me
Becomes a white lie;
I see, on your face,
Light ebbing away;
My veins turn to ice.

❊

Some rages save us, love,
Therefore I raged at you,
And dared you not to move . . .

❊

*Duet for Changing Voices*

The fat got in the fire, dear;
The cat has burned her fur;
What is it you desire, dear?
What is it you desire?

With us, it's either-or, dear,
More often now and then.
A wave climbs toward the shore, dear,
And then falls back again.

I cannot touch your leaves, dear,
The woods have got so thick;
A rose without a thorn, dear,
Is a rose without a prick.
A cat loving a dog, dear,
Just makes herself love-sick . . .

❊

Who'd think a fish pleased in the net?
There are grave secrets to forget,
    The garden is a grave:

This shy one may remember yet
    That we are made for love;
Feeling's a feather. Will she put
    It on before I leave?

❋

Then my bones slowed; I knew
The first faint sense of death,
There, before her,
Heart of my heart, who else
Ever could break my pulse?

❋

The spirit tries to tame
The changes in the sun;
I know the subtle game
Of loving love, alone,
Half in, half out of time,
And stripped to my last skin.

# THE PLAIN SPEECH OF A CROW

## (1954–62)

We sigh before we sing.

*

From off the shore, the plain speech of a crow,
The slow soft heave of surf.

*

If there is not another life, there is at least another way to live.

*

Loneliness is a strange, pitiless teacher.

*

Like the minnow nudging the edge of the water,
Picking the bug-laden surface,
In the world of the skimming dragon-fly,
The thin reeds bent all one way, and the fine grass
Ready to wave at a touch of wind,
Among the white-nosed, black-backed small gold-fish,
The flick-tailed incessant feeders,
The carp of the almost-silent water,
The black fish winking the water,
A slight drift of scum on the green, iridescent water.

*

O I see so little! All that's left is a blind obscure sense of
the earth, a longing to be in another element . . .

*

The circles of my If & When
Dissolving in the rain . . .

❋

The dancers all had dirty feet.

❋

The tree . . .
I saw you come to leaf,
Slow-breather, there outside;
The true shape of my life.

❋

By singing we defend ourselves from what we are.

❋

A ghost grows in this place:
With a fog's filmy ribs,
With a worm's vague face.
I'm lighter on the earth.

❋

Fleeing the heart's blankness, I turned to flowers . . .

❋

All reality sleeps here, in the seed, in the stem . . .

❋

To the Center
All is Near.

❋

The two duties are to lament or praise.

❋

The light dew moistens only those
Ends extended, like the rose,
Drooping beyond the parent stem.
I touch upon a sacred theme:
And leave it living.

✣

I call to what listens:
With the sharp pitch of a bird,
Alone on a singing wire,
As an eye going upward . . .

✣

The air stood up and bristled in my ear.

✣

The pure sound from a tree,
A bird of feather and bone
Sings its extremity . . .

✣

The pert and nimble fancies of a man
Darkened by summer . . .

✣

Walkers at evening pause
Before the exhaling garden,
Giving the flowers their due,
In the oncoming darkness.

Trees keep their shapes: leaves
Rustle a tune of evening,
A sea-wind's sibilant touch
And what always stays.

Before, when buds were younger,
The whistling bare branches
Strained to be elsewhere: away
From the root's anchor.

In this tide of air, the tremor
Of the half-grown roses

Reminds us of the young
And their hapless anger.

Who lives at the dark center
Has his own brightness,
An aura of flame beyond being,
But no answer.

❊

Uncertainly before my eyes,
The branch of this small vision sways
Its budding promise . . .

❊

O for the times when I knew everything!

❊

The peacock and the coyote equally at home.

❊

The moon lolling in a close elm,
The far slope of the range, half light, half shade,
The final man, his bones adrift in fire,
The dream extending beyond darkness and waste,
To see beyond the self
This quiet's but the means,
Whether it's found or lost.

❊

To tell the droll farewell, the final sense
Of what earth is, a place for heavy work,
A place for bees' uninterrupted song.

❊

I see what I believe.

# IN THE LARGE MIND OF LOVE

(1954–62)

So much of me already gone to death.
An old wood rich in glory, a true grave,
A lake with swans in the large mind of love.

✻

The notion of emptiness generates passion.

✻

I stay away from death
By turning toward her face.

✻

I am beside myself, sitting by you.

✻

O Protectress of poets and animals,
O Lighter of miscellaneous fires,
  Shy children of the moon
  Make their way slowly down
  The mountain-face . . .

✻

O my dawn's first dove, I sleep in the dark, the memory of
your kiss a mouthful of sand. For me nothing was granted,
not even Hypocrisy's undulating smile. I embraced a daft cabbage! She was entranced with my obliqueness. What fever
needs is a new mould, an unalterable scum. To the dead,—
which way?

  (Yes, it's possible to create a true natural order simply
by putting things down repeatedly.)

We had Fear for a friend. Even the children are afraid.
Love was a time alone, an incantation of the nose. The
dead lay upside down. A raddled hag. The worse surprise a
corner could have.

When the light sprang back, the town settled into
itself. But the seven sleepers awoke. The woods were aware
of the moaning of the immediate stone. The veery, the fat-
breasted, began whelting the bell of its sorrow. The crow became a goose. No one acknowledged the shudder of the walking bird. All rags flattered the wind.

The mind's eye dawdled, hunting a hole in the wall.

How dare I wave in this necessity, my poor skin and
bones unprotected . . . ?

I lost her sweetness when I looked away, having perceived too narrowly the dry borders of the seen, the coarse,
the handy, the misery, the wind in the bleak hedges of limita-
tion and passion. I in the sweat and stretch of mind spread
too thin; the organ justified the function; the wounds were
fury; the blondes lay in the sand content with themselves in
haphazard America. But it is not true that, as you go West,
life gets more trivial. The places retreat into themselves. (I
saw; I became.) The sand fleas sat. Among the shore-master-
ing weeds, the angel never nests. It's hop and scrape when
the weather dips. *Einfühlung* can go too far. The masters of
nasty congratulated themselves upon having defiled a recently
dead superior. Is Christ so fine? The rat's war is against grain.
Once, children believed it was fun to sit still here.

(Can't we make this discussion a little more disorderly?
I'm not rich but I'm glossy.)

A certain humility before experience is all I ask . . .
Of late you've shocked me truly, with the dins of wow, the
tears of whang. As well to leave me weary, in a dream that
keeps, sweet naught. What I hit with a stick still stares. The
mind's eye hates a wall. But these arching familiars, once lithe
as the bones of a bird, swell to a rigid purpose, determined as a

stone. Is there, after all, an event sweeter than simple seeing? I feel I'm right here. My mother's neighbor gave. Dear Lord, may I be exempted from insects. Do the meek really ever disappear? Indeed I have knees, she said, a high wind over burning water. To know is to love, and the breath of eternity breathes over the sodden field. Slowly the speech of the dead is beaten into praise. An eye walked there, wily as an adder, making a new place pure. Even I can be a mother, giving birth to my father.

❉

What's plain and near? The end of your sweet nose.
I look at you and lapse back into prose.

❉

Love is the true surprise.

❉

The ranges keep their snow.
What lover keeps his song,
The spirit's lonely cry?

Where true beginnings move
The mind, and make their spring.

That shrinking pelt I called
My soul nailed on the door . . .

❉

In the ponds of her being I was the happiest fish;
A cherub dropped in the lap of love.

❉

Her sleek side drying at my side:
This lady cannot leave the room:
She's part and parcel of the pride
That is my doom.

❊

Why should I live in this notebook, already twelve years old,
A child's work, a nineteen-year-old child,
Pleased with herself yet uneasy,—
Yet with an ear! an ear!
And she shakes me now with what she says—
"I began to write when I was quite young.
One day, in the future,—well, I can see that for what it is,
And I know full well that that day will never come.
And so I write usually in the early evening after work and
        school,
And often again before I go to sleep."
Oh my departed mistress, I still see you walking
Down, down, the long dusty corridor.
The lovely, lonely, awkward, unformed, uninformed young
Whom I love too much.

❊

By taking he began to give;
Astonished, found himself in love.

❊

In a place plain as a box,
Her soul found out its work,
Fanning its wings in the dark.

❊

She was, I'd say, most drearily bewitched.

❊

Remember: the gods themselves loathed the furies.

❊

Another time my darling is a dear,
She whispers nothing to my inner ear,
She never kills with kindness, no, not she,
Nor takes advantage of propinquity . . .

✳

I envy the sun at her body.

✳

What's the winter for?
To remember love.

✳

I'm hot for what is.
I take what I touch.

✳

What can I say she is, this thing of light
Morning to midnight haunting my repose,
Breaking my sleep at five, the last of night?

What will abide? I need a morning rose
And knees to bring me to the narrow ridge,
Will-of-the-wood-thing hunting with his nose . . .

✳

I'm sick of women. I want God.

# THE THINGS I STEAL FROM SLEEP

### (1954–62)

Feeling exists in time, and in a dream.
The things I steal from sleep are what I am.

✤

Why is poetry scary?

✤

In truth, the diabolical comes with its desolations,
Its voices, its sulphurous shimmers,
On desert and plain, over the warped bedstead,
The wavering delusional flowers . . .

✤

The minute rages in the clock.

✤

     My bane, my joy,
     My bandy-legged boy,
Came roaring down that manic road . . .

✤

Harvard is not enough.

✤

I walk in this great decay:
The woods wet by the wind,
The dying moss, the brown
Features of time's delay . . .

✤

I seem to be in darkness all the time.

❊

He believes too much, and he knows too much. That's what
    we call mad.

❊

Reared in another place, he came to woe
As to his dinner: it was the thing to do . . .

❊

Shall the gnarled soul
Be reminded again
Of an old motion,
A slapping of water?

❊

I lost what I found
On a dark day,
A mind unsound
In extremity . . .

❊

The mirror told a dirty joke.

❊

A heavenly swearing, tearing off a piece of the wind with
    his wild words . . .

❊

He stretched himself into the greatest good,
Only to break the borders of his mind:
All these went spinning like a cloudy day.

❊

There are brains strewn with nothing but bones.

❊

O.K. You're in agony: make with an agony poem.

❋

Now certain names knock on us like a bell.
Who would believe the meaning of a stick?
There's no one here to tell us we are ill;
The loved adore the loved; the sick the sick . . .

❋

I am undone by knowing what I've done.

❋

Running from God's a long race, and it always ends in a dead
    heat.

❋

For hell is always here: upon the chair
And in these papers strewn upon the floor.

❋

I'm tired. Is that maturity?

❋

Do I stink the rolling air?
This guilt's enough for towns of men:
I keep it navel-tight;
My pride tilting at sticks,
I put this darkness in the air . . .
When shadows start, a changeling steps
Into my dearest dream.

❋

I'm waiting for what I am.

❋

I'm feeling with my feet
To make myself complete.

❋

O God, we're all so full of splits. Can I have Blake cutting an
    orange?

❋

My hair and my ear, my most local condition,
My mile-high meringue, my prodigious pudding . . .
I tasted, and I ate the world.

❋

I once took third place in a hog-calling contest.

❋

I fear I have no mind at all.

❋

O ye motions in air, the chameleons of disorder!
The shape of the mind changes, and we move slow and silvery.
What stamp is on my brow, most particular Toe?
The bright features of lost angels: Yes, yes,
The bright stars say . . .

❋

Something in me doesn't want to be a poet.

❋

I praise myself with howls.

❋

This swarm of swells betrays,
The small trees swirl around,
And only motion stays
And thin wafts of the ground,
The chilly, daft profound . . .

❋

I was not good enough for my own madness.

❋

The birds are going, and their slight songs.
I am ready for a deeper silence.

❋

No way back through the long arbors of the dead.

❋

A desire to love myself in another world . . .

❋

When am I sick? When am I well?
Not even God, I think, could tell.

❋

I feel sorry for the cave, said the Bear.

❋

In his grave he went on dying.

❋

Who loved his life can love his death as well.

# BETWEEN THE SOUL AND FLESH

## (1957)

Between the soul and flesh
What war? I never heard:
I know a singing fish,
A silent bird.

# THE MIRE'S MY HOME

## (1959–63)


The mire's my home! It always was my home.
Fair seed-time had my soul: foul was the edge
Beyond the undulant, the shimmering plain—
Less than the pensive bird, the single man
But half-himself, or something other than.


How can I sleep, a moment from my tears?
Here's all I am: a motion in a shoe
A fish can love: a fish can reach a star
But in this pond there's nothing I can do—
Except to sweat, retch, belch . . .

I carry the curse of many, too many lives.

But this false dawn wakes me only to my own half-life;
I crawl from the miry sheets and the sweat of the drunkard's
    pillow.
I belong back of the barn.
I'm a wave now, part of a journey.
A wave in the false dawn, alas, in the phosphorescence of a tide
    lapsing back.

✳

I dreamt I was a vegetable
    Long as a garden hose;
In self-love all too visible,
    I loved my rooty toes.

I grew beyond the dewy grass,
    I superseded weeds;
I made a planetary fuss
    With my prodigious seeds;

I shook them out upon the plain,
    Across the barren heath;
They sprouted, each and every one,
    Malign, beneath my breath.

They came upon me, coiling worms,
    My being to abuse;
I shrank beneath their hairy arms
    Back to primordial ooze.

And nothing lived: no tree, no bird;
    And no one said alas;
And not a watery bubble stirred
    The place where I once was.

❈

Something is destroying me: I don't know what.

❈

What can I be, now, I've been what I am.
All things remind me of my will to die.

❈

I am but half, who would be whole.

❈

For the madman there is no awakening to a new day: the new day is worse than before, or merely the dark beginnings of another day.

❈

In misery my mould, my life, my time?
Well, then, let misery be truly mine,

the perfect poem is the dead poem:
the language & ...

When the song - sparrows hung
high in the wind,

Above the slant glass, the rain-wet white-wash
~~the~~ the black streaks in the redwood
trying to gray.

The ground needs: the abyss;
We are here because we ... our,
Knowing that
Existence in plain we're not
ontological

I'm praised by fools; ~ Happy polarity ...

the human richness by
Coincidence
The gates swung wide before

Reason unites static & dynamic ... Kingdom of touch this
the anti-literate name - hunters,

It seems odd that a culture ~~seldom~~ addicted to wisdom
in capsules, to digests, to resume, should remain with
The reason is that it is not a ... of a larger thing, but
~~complete~~, or nearly so ... and exist as complete, a
thing, ideally, as the mind, can,

We must have a knowledge that unites:

A ... deep-rooted fear of emotion exists which is
rational enough, since ~~steady~~ emotion among the half-alive
can ... become a danger: is a madness.

The first ... is poetry, particularly lyrical poetry, good
of purity as ... impulse to life perfect. It is one of
the last ways, perhaps the best of not being dead.

Whose lovely unreason

My knees, my knees, that once shapely as a girl's,

~~Was that euphoria a delusion?~~
I ~~remember~~ the day of the dog, when my jaw

And I ran from the cataracts, uphill toward
        lengthened.
    the trails of the forest,

Ran as ~~a man~~ when a child, like a young deer,
    A true Indian

Through the slippery November woods,
    the beech and the bracken,
    And

grieved to say:

    I am bored with the order of a God.

That image came too many times until

What died before me is myself, alone:
~~And~~ him again! Only a man of straw —
Yet straw can feed a fire to melt down stone.

I struggle with my self-deceit; the flaws
~~of straw~~ tricked thinks the self.
Of angels ~~struck~~ my eye. And to ... turn ...
~~And my ...~~ shape thickens, my very own.

I'd have her live with me, an aging wife,
Who tries to live me out of my own life,
Until I dribble at a nerveless chin,
Know neither in from out nor out from in,
A useless one, given to self-abuse,
Afraid of fear, afraid of his own shoes . . .

❈

I'm surrounded by the lint from an enormous navel:
This blare of morning, hideousness of trees tricked out in their chemical greens,
Snot on the walk, and the dead grease of a mineral world.

❈

The slumbering tones in the drum strangled,
The eyeless cloud and the eye of the sun,
The horizon coming upon me.
I speak for myself and my implacable shadow,
For how many months an apparition to myself,
The continual feasts of my mouth appal me,
The arbors, the corridors of honey on the slight hills . . .
The maimed! The maimed! Where is there consolation?
Those who never speak or walk, the twisted,
Reduce my metaphysics to a sigh,
Throw me against the wall, like a gamecock: I need that training.

❈

So much of experience just flows over me: I might as well be a stone at the bottom of a stream: any stone:

❈

I came to a still, but not a deep center,
A point outside the eddying current,
And my eye fastened on a single sand grain,
Neither bright nor dark, on the floor of the river.

❋

All that hunting—for what? A new horror.
Weep out my wants until my eyes are stone.

❋

To remain below life, submerged like a fish frozen in ice.

❋

The dawn's gone for good:
I stare straight at my terror:
The white wind from these petals,
And the cold air whining around my naked ears.

❋

This valediction of the self,
What have I done to prove I am alive?
Things dance in a young mind
Until the soul is blind.

Sometimes it's well to leave things in the air.
Let me remember me: not my despair.

Am I a vanished type, a mastodon
Lunging this way and that in the great damp?

❋

I tire of conscious thought, thinking the will
Will sink into the undimensionable.

❋

The soul's no more at home in this loud place,
A dark shape wrestling with a darker thing,
Father, forgive me, I cried to His Face.
Forgive my words, no longer close to song.
What I once scorned, I secretly embrace.

Teach me, sweet love, a way of being plain!
My virtues are but vices in disguise,
The little light I had was Henry Vaughan's.
I hunted fire in ice: the soul's unease
In the loose rubble, the least glittering stone:
And what I found was but one riddled bone:

I move, unseeing, toward an absolute
So bright within it darkens all I am;
Am dropped away: dropped out of time,
One still too frail to bear himself, alone . . .

✻

For he could love the world, but not himself;
And cried to be an instrument. And was.

✻

All roads lead to the self:
Hug me, O shirt of fire.
The little light I share
Is gone: I am nowhere . . .

✻

Mother of God, deliver me to me . . .

✻

All things rolling away from me,
All shapes, all stones,
My face falling from itself,
Sunken, like cratered snow,
My voice, lost, a lark
Grating like a jay.
As for you, assassin of air,
Noise in the topmost tree,
Articulated despair,

The inhuman ecstasy:
My lament to the last; unloved . . .

*

I, in exile, forever
For that which I would acquire no longer is, never existed.

*

I belong to my solitude.
I shall die for myself.

# THE DESOLATION

(1959–63)

She wrapped me in her breath;
She wound me dilly-down:
Easy to die the death
As bone against bone.
      —She's mine! She's mine!
      Parsley, vetch, and thyme:
      And the moon, the moon down
      Into the lap of time.

✻

She. Woman's the noble word for the bright soul.
He. Things as they are beat at me like a flail.
She. Deep dreamless sleep is true beatitude.
He. Or frenzy called up by a gush of blood.

✻

Beware of me, love:
My deer leaping's dangerous,
My shrieking above
The infernal clatter of the storm
Will drop to a quaver after
The thunder
Rolls away from the hill-top
And the tip of the pine
Lashes back, half-broken;
I'll have taken
More than myself away
From you and your childish
Beguilings, your rose-bow

Of a mouth, your nose
Pert as a bird's, and your
Quail-like shying
Before surrendering more
Than I ever gave:
I'll be gone, love.
In late autumn, you came
Running after me, as if
I were game to be shaken
Out of the underbrush by a retriever,
Tail-pointing: but the game's over,
Now you are the hunted, the haunted.

❖

Does she scream or bleat
Or plant her feet
    On the ceiling, with a frown?
Does she leave you there,
Still up in the air
    Or let you slowly down?

❖

The bed denies me, the floor accepts me.

❖

I assumed another sex; I acquired the pure limpidity of a prince
    of life;
I witnessed the triumph of plumbing, in a place where God
    suffered;
I stepped close to a swirling fire, in a daze of love-longing,
Unwearied by my minor elations, my dreadful joys, my flaked
    skin,
In the ample bosom of poverty, I lay, serene as a leaf on a wave,
A crumb lively in the lap of love.

❖

Bride of my silence, I am no bridegroom . . .

❋

Her ear, still back in a deep cave,
Hearing the boom of the long surf at the foot of a cliff,
A breeze from the sill on her eyelids,
Her arm, almost ready to move—
Her hair piled like the lair of a meadow-mouse,
Or a rain-beaten nest of a wren, in September—
How can I stay silent in this twilight
When one shift of my weight explodes the tin bed,
And wakes her, raging.

❋

Sing halla loo and how d'ye hoo
    The pudding and the pie:
I had a wife, and whadd'ye think
    She thinks I have to die.

❋

Where is my love, my Marguerite, my mind
To end all minds that leaves but human love?
I cannot see your image for my eyes.
Love's lethal mixture makes for mutual hate.

❋

The furies laughed to see
Our spectres, eye to eye—
The desolation of our felicity.

❋

Since you'll never know my wish,
Why should I pine and sigh
Until love's beaten from my flesh
And I am no longer I
But a shape rooting through a hedge,
Escaped from the sty?

Soul, take my flesh and know,
Flesh, take my soul and flee
For my soul's ecstasy
Is no saint's privilege.
What would you, love? I know
That sensual ecstasy
Is but the will to die . . .

*

I read in forgotten books
The passionate interplay
When lovers come to a choice,
Throw themselves away.
Their way is not for me.
My today is more than today,
And I look with a hunter's eye
Toward eternity.

# MY FLESH LEARNED TO DIE

## (1959–63)

At the edge of my horror I sat, a worn child, a soul desiring to
      return—
To what? To the shape of its father or mother?
Faced by myself, what else could I do?

*

Creating from denial what I can,
Conquest of suffering brings back such joy,
I am a child again, a brainless boy.

*

I would be with the wind, in the thump and slam of this
      summer joy.

*

I learn by the way of the fool,
The moth, and the child,
My two eyes embracing all,
Ingenuous, wild.

*

As we age, we change our ways of rejoicing,
No longer able to meet the wind at the hilltop,
Or race over stony ground, like the goat or the puppy,
Or snatch at fireflies blinking on and off in the damp grass.

*

She of the parched garden,
She holding the hoe in gnarled hands,
She sweating beneath wrinkled eyelids,

A hag among weeds,
Once a glory to waves, rippling back the sun,
A delight to battered walls, wood broken,
The change of evening among ancient ferns,
She who believed my hands,
Who despaired of my dying.

✽

Which door?
I can't here.
Her thighs
Were my shoes
For leaping away.

That's something to know:
The berry bright skin
Takes only one in:
Her garden, her mound
Was but the harsh ground
Where my flesh learned to die—
And I saw the dark beast
Of myself, chained and wild . . .

✽

Some day, my while, tell me what time's like?—
A fat load on a slow cart, or a child's romp with the wind.
For you see I have gone to the edge of my extent,
The fringe of my worst delight,
Bedunged, beslimed, bedevilled and bedamned.

✽

Staggering between the madhouse and the grave.

✽

I live in a country,
The land of the free—
Did I eat my mother

Or did she eat me?
Or was the devouring
Done mutually?
I cherish her image
When I look in the glass,
I was a true son:
Of the middle-class.
But now shapes and shadows
Throng the stair and the hall
And I lie thinking
Nothing at all, nothing at all.
Outside, the slow winds
Move through the long grass,
Where my father keeps moaning
Alas, alas.

*

I know how flowers think. Behold in me
One who transcends the sensual ecstasy.
By grubbing among stones, in the close dirt,
I found out where my father left his heart . . .

*

Where my lost father is: there would I be.

# AND TIME SLOWS DOWN

## (1960–63)

Ceaseless the action of the water:
The little nudgings of the tide into the tiny rock-craters,
The waves like the skin of a fish,
Small, close, and all alike:
Then a sudden cross-riffle of wind changes all to a diagonal
      fluttering.

Then almost silence, almost a pond-shimmer.

A leaf falls on the sheep-path,
Loud as a step.
Another drops into the water,
Rides like a child's boat on the green debris, stiff as a shell,
Stiff as a broken nut-shell, floating
The undulant inch-long waves wrinkling toward me . . .

And time slows down, slows down.
The vine-like dead branches of the madrona arch over the
      water,
Creaking slightly with each light wind-shift;
The wave-shimmers play back on the parched leaves.

*

The confraternity of beach and wave,
The slow sea swell that never breaks on the shore,
The wave-rippled sand, the unattainable . . .

*

Like the paper birch I delight in the company of conifers and
      the presence of water.

*

The mountain looms, the mother,
Its ranked trees taking, changing the light,
Alder glittering like magnolia,
Waxy even in the far haze.

Pine leans on pine, the trees thinner;
Two bald eagles fly around the bend of a river,
A thin blue smoke rising from a sawdust furnace,
A gandy-dancer sleeps in the half-grown ferns,
A hundred hawks ride motionless, down a wind current.

Where green changes to mossy stone, and the last snow of the
    mountain,
The clay banks crumbling back, the long reeds leaning all one
    way, loose as whips;
A white pail on a fence-post, its bottom rusted deep brown;
The brown cows among the black stumps;
The green moss and the brown;
The dead fir, all its silver branches curved down . . .

At last I ride, almost as if upon water,
Lurching slightly, hearing no longer the drone of the fan,
But only the wheels clicking beneath,
Rejoicing in these sudden vistas of flat water,
Between the high bluffs,
The little ponds with their ducks in the corner of the wheat
    field.

And it all seems to have meaning, even the broken machinery,
The abandoned oil wells, the rowboat sunk in the ice of
    winter . . .
Is this waste, this debris a necessary part of our energy? . . .

The route of the eagle changes with the wind;
The thin green grass grows up over the sloping rubble,

The wing-stem flower rises out of the cleft of rock
Near a rubble of stones, and light-green grass of a tilted hillside,
The star shapes widen on the small stems,
And the rich brown center of a dried log breaks open . . .

And all shapes alter within, like a layer of snow under pressure,
Thinner and finer than the tip of a dead pine, wind-sharpened,
And I am one with a line of black pipes climbing a yellow road,
With that cub bear making his own snow-balls,
And the little brown log riding the ripples, live as a fish,
And the hawk hunting low over his valley, pure as a pigeon,
The water trickling down over the perpendicular rock-face;
The dead silvery trees, like uplifted driftwood . . .

✳

I like to sit in the dark like that splintery pine growing into the
    rock.

✳

We take from nature what we cannot see.

# THE THIN CRIES OF THE SPIRIT

## (1959–63)

The beginning's not the deed:
The flowering's but the seed.
It is ourselves we need.

The spheres themselves consumed
In a darkening room—
Yet where's the sense of doom?

My haunted ancestors
Peer down from the stray stars,
From their lost everywheres,

Saying, you should be this.

*

What's my blood? Worse.
Where's the white? Now.
Who's to know? You.
Keep the nest: near . . .

*

I would put myself, pit myself against oblivion.

*

The sense something is pushing from within: the whole being
in motion: a force almost too much for the frame of bones;
a sense related to the drive toward multiplicity: a reaching
out to all sights, aware of sound—so aware that the sudden
noise makes one jump as if it were the blast of a .45—the

car horn's an agony. It is indeed a special kind of tension:
the hand shakes in writing, and often trails off in a scribble . . .

❈

I do not own reality, he said,
Acting as if he did.

❈

O which reality is yours?
Whatever slides, whatever pours.

❈

An eternal death-watch, this gazing at the sea,
A midge on my page.
Perpetuation of what should be silent,
The fox and the crow are reconciled . . .
The angels of light have forgotten how to fly:
I have lost a shadow.
What rules, what measures for my own being?
Those ignorant of why they live—rarely love . . .

❈

Whether there's motion in that sodden will,
In that dark turbulence, where fallen spirits quail,
Leviathan, I feel thy heavy name:
Fate of these symbols, cast upon the floor,
Let motion in its tiny center sit;
The belly eats itself.

❈

I am indeed pinned by the arrows of vainglory,
Transfixed by this mirror of imperfect lucidity,
The Devil needs new life: Let's give him some.
By gazing away, we enter more deeply into ourselves.

❈

My rage, where's the edge
Of the fine thought

I carried so long?
My wrath, what's to be?
Have I lost my own name
In the trash, in the stones?
And winter shivers
My spine now,
In the dry earthy air.

I have been too long a Laocoön of my own entrails.

❊

Is this our loss, the last reality,
The imagination, that hawk, that prowling bird,
That kingfisher on the bank of our astonishment,
Its eye and beak hungry for new waters,
Diving at the least sign, or glitter from the muddy depths,
To emerge, lifting its catch in the sunlight.

❊

As lungs know the air, lungs a part of this body,
This machine I have almost destroyed, given to me for safe-
        keeping,
So a part, only a part, of the body comprehends the spirit,
And I climb the hill, not breathless, yet with love-longing
        of a kind,
The kind the child knows on a too-high branch of a tree,
Tilting crazily away from the shrieks of his mother, the eyes
        of his neighbor.

❊

The cicada plucks at a single string, diminishing,
My heart beats with the grass, the slime-silvered stones,
In the great void of space there is an answer . . .
O the thin cries of the spirit, the tiny landscape of the
        migratory souls!
Blood from the hawk's beak, blood from the guts of the
        crushed mouse,

Myself and the air!
The gliding birds never denying their element.
Is it all the same
Out of me, out of me,
The pure bird on its stone . . .

*

What I lost in a trance, my senses saved.

*

What news? What news to meet the solemn day;
Weight of all being and all things afresh,
Terror and joy in close identity.
The sea behind the wave, the shore awash
With a great welter of dead kelp and stones
While all I am speaks out—in undertones.

*

And I'll go down to the dark
Where the last shadows talk,
And the wind-ripped tree abides
Alone, with its ragged birds.

# MY INSTANT OF FOREVER

(1959–63)

I implore with both hands: to the best of myself I pray, my faith an entrance into the whole of reality.

Like Adam, I sacrifice the unicorn in place of myself, and like Plato, remain ingloriously silent.

In the face of a mystery I cannot shake loose.

In this almost-life, I tremble at the wrist, at the waist; and my belly eats me, never refuses to cherish its own peculiar odor.

Like that St. Francis of the will to power, I need eternity; I have no thread of purpose left; I crave for Apollo's eyes, the Dionysian heart,

Like that prating ass Goethe, I rejoice in the rationally incomprehensible.

I love him, in concealment, the spirit of life trembling in one lip like a ripple in still waters.

✲

Now what to do, sweet Jesus, what to do?
Each child corrupted by the virgin's smile,
Monstrous confusion in the burning heart
Of God himself: Sweet Jesus, what do we do?
I am a man, a man without a name,
A prisoner in time, in this foul time.
All contradictions poised to fly apart,
Children in love with death: before their time.
Jesus of cripples, cry out in my name;
Only the abyss is real, and that's defiled
By the raw stench of hell; where, where's my God

That led me partly up this stony path,
I would receive the full blow of his wrath:
But there's no wrath: only this vertigo,
No heavenly scourge, nor dire abrasive blast.

❉

My bones shrink to a bird;
I am less than a child,
A vein beating, unheard,
In the close, in the coming dark,
My spirit turns to its work.

❉

That ultimate seed, the soul,
Growing between two stones,
Heard a mandrake's groans,
A sound altering all
Bird-songs and bird-bones . . .

❉

A hurry's been put upon me, a deep urge
To live beyond my life, on the true edge
Of what all things would be—
To sail beyond all sensual ecstasy
As if a stone had flowered to a bird.

And yet I grope among these broken stones,
A mangy dog snuffling at pitted bones.

❉

Have I become a spiritual man?
To this dark place I've come, and come again
As if led by my nose . . .
A bald two-legged hound
Sniffing the mouldy ground
In a blind search.
I left my hat some place, and then my pen:

My breathing is not easy as it was:
Still searching out unsearchable repose.

*

In those pages I sense an awareness of raw stones,
In this intolerable sadness of longing too much—
Of not knowing what it is I love.

*

I ask a question of the supernatural.
At what point does the self become the soul
When it deserts this clumsy animal,
This bear-like shape that lumbers down a hall
Or clambers up a hill?

*

I went into a flame,
A priest of kingdom come,
The false light cried my name,
"You are no one."

I saw a shape in a crowd,
Grisly, amorphous, lewd;
I cried, and loud,
"Here! Here is our God!"

A pure light came;
And stole me away
From time.

*

In the hot sweat of why not,
In the cold dark of who did,
In the battered dish of she dares
In the absolute dead middle of all-around
—I dug my flesh until I was a wound
    And the day sighed out its light, and the white kingdom
        came.

*

Outside time
Beyond the forms of this dark,
Give me one pulse of that heart,
One push from those lungs,
One touch of his ribs,
And I'd dive into the bright
Heart of the night, I'd take on
With the thin bones of my hands
Every weak weed of my life. Their petals fall
To the ground before his imagined shadow.
I am neither near nor far, nowhere in time,
O now nothing but hasps and needles,
With a young snake's tongue to rise an inch from his face:
Only that air he breathes,
With the flaming heart
Of a heart . . .

Battle my bones, you bars, I'm here to stay
While the light falls through the rain on the raw
Hills of my promise,
Let others judge my case.

One mad for knowing I am. One of the young
With a crippled will, a nose like a broken potato,
And he gave me a cripple's mien,
Staring beyond me, into the half-light of the late afternoon,
Where two gulls walked, fatter than geese,
Now once for the living I sing and twice for the dead,
And three times for that mad thing that rules the world of
         my loose will
To be all and nothing at once.
Grant me that for a split
Instant this side of hell.

✤

The human soul does not live, but is life, the life of the body.

✤

Innocency renewed:
The soul talking to itself in the long silences,
After the feathery rain plumes the high fir-trees,
And the waves lapse back,
And the morning mists begin moving over the low marshes,
To the best of myself I prayed:
Was that enough?
In that cold glittering, the last of light,
In the clarity of thumping substances,
The glare and blare drowning the soul's voice,
I sank deep into my bones;
My eyes opened inwardly to the small light,
The unconsuming fire outlives the wind;
I remembered what I was.

✤

I have partaken of the heavenly food;
I have received the message from the place of perfection—
But what do I do now, facing the foam
On the shore, under the parched madrona with its crown of
        birds—
Let the moon walk over me? I have found my deeper life.

✤

This man, longing for God,
I who spent all a sad childhood longing for the sea,
Delight in my crown of birds, a god for an instant,
My instant of forever.

✤

May my words leap lightly on the tongues of laughing men,
And a laughing God receive me

To another, brighter beginning,
After a sudden end . . .

\*

I'm dead awake, thank God.

\*

What I have, whole,
Whom I know, loved.

I, who was half-defined,
Came to another mind.
The pure final repose
Of the widening rose.

When I think of an time Rilke had, I could
weep: and the things about him which
tied him to the past and helped make
him human.

— ~~~

~~Made no humour a~~
poet make me human, again!
~~A~~ God in myself would be too much!
~~No~~
~~it won't~~
it's not ~~far~~
~~just some will carry me~~!

Let me see its face, that will stalking me,
Or does it live in mirrors like the eye,
Baleful ~~~~~

One others ~~it~~ integrated. [Eternal
The quieting of ~~separate~~ is words of my.
Art is too important for anonymity!
invented in some situations; my or ~~coercions~~ or memory
Malice, ~~under con~~

My most desperate efforts to be friendly is to
tell someone I value them in some way.
— ~~~ —

This may be an oblique discussion of a
problem that does not exist.

The moon played on her ever-whitening brow:
Her temples said: _____ is snow

Another journey gone? You're always going on
The moon on an ever-whitening brow, journey.

I have received the message from the place of
I have partaken of the heavenly perfection;
A man paying his tribute in cochineal and like
etc.

But _____ I want to die now, facing _____ eating
for the edge of a possible heaven?—
Stretch into a deep sleep,
On the shore under the punished umbrance,
Let the moon walk over me?

In hope's light time,
The _____ soul leaves with the _____.
_____ he leaves mirrors on this line,

_____

In hell is always here;
In the _____ in the dark brown battlefield
& to my longevity

# PROSE

# ALL MY LIGHTS GO DARK

(1943–47)

The first snow transformed the whole field. The ploughed loam, with its high ridges left black. One bird in the center of a tree.

The snow began coming straight down, almost like a rain: gray.

A tree like an inverted broom.

An intricate fine bush close to the window.

All the knobs of incidental design.

That sense: here I belong—so rare.

Inner nervousness: as if my entrails were grinding and about to fly off in parts.

A brown field, dusted with snow, turns to a light yellow.

An in-between time, before the complete harsh glittering whiteness: a purgatorial world, a netherworld.

*

Seminal states of waiting, a sacramental view of nature, listening to wind-sounds, looking at snow in a far-away field.

*

A sense that from each image some profound truth might be grasped.

*

The feeling that one is on the edge of many things: that there are many worlds from which we are separated by only a film; that a flick of the wrist, a turn of the body another way will bring us to a new world. It is more than a perpetual expectation: yet sometimes the sense of richness is haunting:

it is richness and yet denial, this living a half a step, as it were, from what one should be. The valleys are always green, but only the eyes, never the feet, are there . . . The feeling is always with us, but most in the middle morning.

✱

How are you this morning?—the eternal question.

✱

I have mercy in the morning.

✱

First I must look, then I must learn.

✱

A morning without precedent: everything, absolutely everything covered with a light, almost blue frost. The sun came up over the mountain through a yellowish yet intense haze. There was a light snow on the ground. The pipes sang their light song.

✱

I love the first movement of a snow storm over the fields, especially when there has not been much previous snow, at least not enough to break down the weeds. The discovery that comes at last: that the self, which seemed so marvellous and inexhaustible, was really desolate and barren; so I suppose that is why I love the snow, this morning, after working without result all night.

✱

How garish and terrible a car looks in a winter countryside, with all its natural purity.

✱

An over-particularized place sense: *why* do we want to be in one chair at one time of day, particularly . . . ?

✤

My memory, my prison.

✤

I am nothing but what I remember.

✤

Intense inner life: I remember watching a solitary walker often, as a child, feeling sorry for him. If it is true that one's basic character is established in quite early childhood, then I still have a chance.

✤

How involved with others, even the stranger on the street, in living! How much of our imagination he takes up. We see an eye, or a breast, or a muscled calf: we remember a particular toothiness—there is a desire to be of them. Like leaf-desiring worms we turn our eyes: we reach and fumble in those gestures of half-love.

✤

At that time the significance of small acts . . . even an old carpet was a dazzle of scenes, and the clock never told me more; a turn of the head a panorama of difference.

✤

What an aura lay upon all experience at the time when the merest act, the lightest finger, the barest raising of the brow, was suffused with tenderness.

✤

Close to the central mysteriousness of life he was, the times in childhood when existence seemed fraught with the greatest possibilities: in a June night, out on the sleeping porch.

✤

Greenhouse appeared in a dream as a sparkle of glass: like dream of flat water: the calm, the eye of a pond.

✤

What was the greenhouse? It was a jungle, and it was paradise;
it was order and disorder: Was it an escape? No, for it was
a reality harsher than reality.

✤

The long mind roves back.
I wear between my eyes the image of death.
I carry death in my mouth.

Blundering man, gentle with birds,
Whom the caterpillar caressed,
Whom the snake kissed.

I was never his son, not I.

✤

I sank into the womb of the barn,
Grain scraping my soft underarms;
I lay under the benches, breathing with weeds,
Snails in my hair,
Weed-blistered, bloody-kneed,
Cursing my father's life,
Outcast who spit in the well,
Dropped like hay down the chute . . .

✤

I was born under a glass heel and have always lived there.

✤

I wish I could photosynthesize.

✤

The flower's by-its-selfness.

✤

Only the dead luxuriate.

❊

The terrible energy of the dead.

❊

There is a time almost the same, in spring and in fall, when the mould seems to sprout its own announcements, when the dead detritus speaks only of life.

❊

Loveless one, in despair you shall be learned.

❊

Reaching out more desperately for life. Training himself to love life.

❊

More than a feeling: a desire for the qualities in primitive forms of life: crabs, snails—

❊

The leading under-the-stone poet of our time.

❊

Long, fruitless introspection, characteristic of the German, relieved by occasional dim flickers of insight. Like a half-blind animal that at best can see no colors but gray, he broods and broods.

❊

Teetering precariously on the brink of the navel.

❊

Many meditations destroy.

❊

A love for the bottoms, the fell last roots of things.

❊

The sense of aloneness sometimes accompanied by a kind of mindless brooding, looking fixedly at sticks, old grass . . .

✣

The self must be a bridge, not a pit.

✣

The crater of hell: the navel.

✣

I think as I smell.

✣

I like to think a thing part way through and feel the rest of the way.

✣

I'm beginning to see myself in perspective: how I set too great a store on the simple and sensuous.

✣

After a time people will tire of my threshing out of a marsh.

✣

For the innocent eye in the mature man makes a false kingdom of the spirit.
My soul must dwell for a time in dark places;
My ears must listen intently for the clapping of hands.

✣

Sometimes a relish with which he contemplated his own stupidity.

✣

I'd like to have my sensibility violated—even raped—by an idea sometime.

✣

He constantly was preparing himself to survive boredom.

✣

Seized by an attack of boredom, in this preserve, as acute as peritonitis.

✤

The sense: I should be somewhere else. The teeth always slightly grinding.

✤

Always basing my life on the intangible, the impossible.

✤

At first a terrible depression, the sense again of impending disaster: a mixture, alternate exaltation and despair coming closer.

✤

I spent my life doing things I keep trying to forget.

✤

The new resolutions: I will take walks, start a new notebook, work with my hands.

What *am* I worrying about?

Why do I hunt for something to hate, for something to annoy me?

How terrible the need for God.

The paradox of destruction: I can no longer be good— I am bored with the moral course, yet anything otherwise produces anxiety.

A gnawing nervousness of one who has learned to keep down the worst concomitants . . .

The state of wanting to kill everything one loves: cut off more than the nose to spite the race.

To wish for an illness—for something to come to grips with, a break from reality.

Or to eat—and again to forget.

Life ". . . a mockery of ragged ends . . . an irrational bitterness . . ."—A. G. Gardiner.

Exasperation.

❖

That exhaustion, as if the top of the mind were sewn by strong thread, with just enough give to permit me to wrinkle my forehead.

❖

No longer unhappy, but filled with an intolerable sadness: not nostalgia. At least self-pity can be enjoyed: misery, a true state, cannot.

❖

. . . A cold paralyzing horror: a glimpse into the subhuman . . . The sickness of life beginning again: the exhausting awareness of every ache. What the hand does in reaching, a misery of awareness; loss of memory in small things; hatred of necessary routines; hatred but not fear of dark; watching the skin, the fingers; overeating; a full preoccupation with unnecessary tasks; weakness in the morning; fear of headlights; distrust of children; a tide of loss.

❖

The intolerable sadness that comes when we are aware at last of our own destiny.

❖

To be weary of one's own individuality—is that to die?

❖

For Lawrence and I are going the same way: down:
A loosening into the dark, a fine spume-drift,
The touch of waters: the dark whorls, the curled eddies.

❖

My vision falling like a burning house.

❖

Who, when he was born, eclipsed all living; wished himself blind so he could see nothing but himself.

❖

The visible exhausts me. I am dissolved in shadow.

❖

Slow as a potato eye seeking a crack . . .

❖

I had just gone out to the icebox to replenish my intuitions.

❖

My feelings lagging behind like a small dog.

❖

He has several bad habits: eating, drinking, and breathing.

❖

Drink, coffee, cigar. Or cigar, coffee, drink. Or cigar, drink, coffee—or—?

❖

Whenever I drink or the wind blows, I think.

❖

Living as if everything were slightly a-tilt.

❖

How bleak and black and dead-ended can be the literal approach to experience: the eye is *not* enough.

❖

A sick man learns from silence.

❖

Warning of lint and warped windows. Villages age early under snow. Oiled babies. Fetor of hearts at the edge of the

city . . . Smother myself in the arms of a shadow. Fly out
of doors, clown of mediocrity . . . A lovely clear lucid drunken-
ness.

*

If we are too violent in escaping from one trap, we fall into
another.

*

I have contempt of the self, but still indulge it like a fond
mother.

*

Now for you I shall perform a set of tumble-ditties and scamper-
songs fit to delight the dead.

*

The divided man becomes
Mother and child at once.

*

Saw the mirrors in two.
I'm a divided man.
The little I try to do
Is less than I can.

*

O the hideousness of second-class mail and mirrors!

*

My second-best shape,
Doll, calf, or baby,
I love you best
In the first of morning . . .

*

Reason, keep away from my door.

❋

To know one's limitations, that's what modern heroism consists of, says someone. Not to know one's limitations: madness.

❋

I said to the cat, "I'm the most elemental thing in this room!"
It ran up the wall.

❋

All ear and no brain
Make Teddy inane.

❋

I am more than my skin allows.

❋

My manias walking in their blaze.
May all your hushes be prodigious.

❋

Body drags soul into the changeable.

❋

Euphoria: the waste in it; the bounding animal energy flowing
into every vein.

❋

If I feel good, I can't think.

❋

I love my follies.

❋

"I'm going to be a great man," he cried. "A minor hint of a
great man; but still great."

❋

The dangerous notion that one's secret wish will direct events.

❊

The ecstasy. Supersensuous state: violently visited. There is
no end to the worlds even here. Can there be a higher state
than this? But there are many states toward it. And a violent
going high and going low. Blake, too, was not of the type to
let slip what he had learned.

❊

I am the edge of an important shadow.

❊

And the resemblance, that I can tell you, is accidental.
The tears, for instance, are quite human;
Only when he begins walking do we see the difference,
There is a rolling gait, decidedly anthropoidal,
And a twist in the hips denoting the premature loss of a tail.
If you will state the sources of his income, I can give you
       my conclusions tomorrow.

❊

Are we closest to knowledge when we are farthest from the body?

❊

Lord of Laughter and Light, attend me.

❊

The Exhorting of Everything: wanting to make the woods move,
the birds sing, the world to be alive with one's own aliveness.

❊

God robbed poets of their minds that they might be made
expressions of his own.

❊

The Second Terror: (at realization of age, of disintegration,
of time.) Going in and out of time: not as if going in and
out of a stream; but as in breathing: the hot ashy air from
a blast furnace.

✤

One attitude: "I am damned. Therefore I must live as desperately as possible, for this will be the end of me."

✤

At last there came a time when there was no longer a point in being a horse.

✤

You can't be excited about going to sleep.

✤

I should be honored I should be pardoned I should be alone I should be dead.

✤

A light wind keeps waking me. My handwriting grows more crabbed and secret.

✤

Have you said all yourself, poor stir-fire, rack-rent heart . . . ?

✤

I am hoarse from silence.

✤

All my lights go dark. I fold into black stone.

✤

All forms darken. Things cannot know us.

# THE CAT IN THE CLASSROOM

## (1943–47)

In the classroom, as instinctive as a cat and as restless.

✻

A too explicit elucidation in education destroys much of the pleasure of learning. There should be room for sly hinters, masters of suggestion.

✻

I have a jumbled mind that only achieves clarification at times and then under pressure, as in a classroom. Then the material provides the unity; the random insights.

✻

Therefore I shall get on with the daily business of revelation.

✻

He's got to want to teach in the same way as in the old days a preacher wanted to preach. Historically, there are analogies here; many of the men who once went into the church now go into teaching . . .

✻

I miss the administrator who will hammer the table and say, "Everything's been organized: we want to disorganize it. We want intense people who can teach."

✻

By suggestion, by insinuation, by intuition—let the material speak for itself: elucidate quietly. There's a short-hand in teaching just as there is in poetry. I smell out my material like an old she-bear.

❉

There is a kind of teaching short-hand: a possibility of suggestion which can be far more powerful than the ablest analysis: for analysis is, after all, a negative function . . . To make them feel *and* think simultaneously. To make the thought as real as the sight and smell of a rose: the growth of the student who can be reached in this way is much more rapid.

❉

To teach men to flourish: to press my sensualism into a seed—how can I?

❉

At adolescence: so much they don't know; but, in the case of the best of them, what they do know is important and often lost to us later.

❉

Those taught to creep become enchanted with such locomotion.

❉

Teacher: a capacity for enthusiasm about the obvious.

❉

Men are made by books.

❉

Very few whose conversation is intelligent or even lively: yet a few who live in the element who can make even the shabbiest cliché sound exciting.

❉

There's not enough random energy around here. Nothing but horse sense at work.

❉

That mass education sacrifices the best is a platitude; but the extent to which the young, the best of the young, are sold out, are misled, are ignored . . . The shallow egotists, the empty exhibitionists . . . the trimmer, the bootlicker, the hot-air merchants, the angle-boys have taken over.

✤

If you only knew how cold and merciless, fishy and thoroughly bad so many institutions are.

✤

The teaching profession: too many clever men without any gifts other than a low cunning; too many cardinal's secretaries.

✤

Teaching: the great crime is lack of a generous mind.

✤

Those dear delicious swoons of nerves, praters combining all the worst features of goose and parrot; the patters of their own dung, writhing out tiny noises; instructors of a deep contempt, hucksters of others' talent, rabbits in hutches of mis-conception, moles—weak-eyed—professors of no love, masters of sterilized ritual and organized self-deception—keep me from these evils, Lord, and the rest I'll take care of myself.

✤

Prayer: Dear Lord, may I never become one of those soft-faced sleek self-loving academic eunuchs, from whom all sharp-ness and cunning have fled, in self-created vacuity.

✤

He was a man with little capacity for any kind of thinking: therefore he was made an administrator.

✤

A rat-trap sensibility: slams down on subject, maims and kills it but retains it.

✤

Teaching goes on in spite of the administrators.

✻

I teach naturally; a student is a supplement to me, like a wife is to some men.

✻

Teaching: I am against realities at one or two removes, the imposing of the second-hand.

✻

Richness of personal nature, even without "brains," can produce good teaching.

✻

Our ignorance is so colossal that it gives me a positive pleasure to contemplate it.

✻

A curious physical tremor, a thrill at seeing something done badly.

✻

The secret admiration we have for anything done well, even murder.

✻

I've had few students who can read a fresh page. Reason: this can be taught only by parents. One reason is that the exclamation point and question mark are the only devices we have for inflection . . . What we ought to teach is the right way to use the voice. Teach them to read with their ears as well as their eyes . . . We must teach them the sacredness of human communication.

✻

A teacher: to bridge those terrible gulfs that lie often between personalities.

✻

Not the boring moments, the small gratifications, but the struggle where we become something more than shadows.

✻

All the time you're in here something is supposed to be going on: you're not just sitting there, you're not receptacles, little vessels into which I pour something: our insights are mutual.

✻

I had all this feeling of love for everybody and then when I got there, I set my teeth.

✻

Maybe in love I'm just a teacher too.

✻

The element of self-destructiveness in teaching.

✻

The damage of teaching: the constant contact with the un-developed.

✻

Going to Bennington a little like going into the Marines.

✻

Cold heart, stone heart, cold-of-a-cold peace-heart,
Everybody to take a piece of my poor quivering sensibility.

✻

The harshness of his way of life, the constant projection of his most intimate self, the dramatization—all these left him tired . . . All he wanted was to be alone. In his dingy solitude of a cheap lamp, and quiet.

✻

Teacher: one who carries on his education in public.

✢

I like to teach because I like to see people part of the day.

✢

Those black hours when he feels that he has dispersed himself on the air.

✢

Gradually a pile of student papers begins to smell like old meat.

✢

My frenzied example. It's been a long semester here at Hysteria Hall. My intense and vexed superficiality.

✢

I will recite my mistakes:
1) I have overstressed the medium.
2) I have indulged in gags.
3) I have traded and trumpeted.

✢

I can't abide you unless you talk back. I hope for your hearts. I wait for you. I wish for you. I can believe my heart a certain time. I wish for you, *bambini* of the nerves.

✢

Through the young, I shall recover my lost innocence.

# THE TURN OF THE WHEEL

## (1943–47)

But in the life of one man, never
The same returns. Sever
The cord, shed the scale. Only
The fool, fixed in his folly, may think
He can turn the wheel on which he turns.

✻

The passage of time: a man floating straight up; swirling as in a very swift river.

✻

Step out of time as stepping out of water, a low stream winding through a pasture.

✻

I dropped my watch into the stream of time.

✻

It's the before and after of time that I hate.

✻

I do not wish a sense of the past: only a sense of the continuous.

✻

Today anyone who thinks about what matters is "tortured."

✻

One of those people who have been busy all their lives trying to destroy themselves; who have a sufficient self-contempt and detachment to acquire a curious kind of warped objectivity in viewpoint and, also, their own kind of wisdom.

✻

A philosopher is one who worries and worries about the obvious.

✻

Why not hate everybody? he said. It's a good sound philosophical position.

✻

My great truth: it is possible to love the human race.

✻

I flee into life: escape to a face from the page.

✻

The only time I feel a sense of kinship with people is at the movies or in the bus on the last ride.

✻

All relationships are between commodities: I have been wooed and won by a package of Quaker Oats.

✻

Love: looks and sounds like murder.

✻

For I believe the spiritual combat to be more desperate in the center of chaos, which is Detroit.

✻

Those Catholic pictures always scared the living Jesus out of me.

✻

The *fun* (not just pleasure) certain temperaments get in exhortation to virtue.

✻

At least I have a sense of evil: that's more than most possess.

✻

The Fall of Man, as the Bible recounts it, is really the Fall of God.

✻

I'd like to take every saint and personally re-fry him.

✻

What am I, a spiritual gigolo?

✻

Who gave squalor a style and chaos a human look?

✻

Wait. Watch. Listen. Meditate. He'll come. When? No, I know He won't come. He doesn't care about me any more. No, I mean Him, the Big He, that great big three-cornered Papa.

Will He be wearing a three-cornered hat,
Will He walk up the street just like that,
Will He play with the birds
Or roll in the turds . . .
Will He sing with the girls in the choir,
Will He say, You may have your desire,
Will He play at football,
Will He smirk in the hall,
Now tell me: I'm mad to know *what*.

✻

There are few things a thinking man can be certain of. The God of his childhood will change to something else.

❖

What is the necessity for worship? To *praise* God. Surely if
that is the case, most good humans transcend God for they do
not wish praise.

❖

A rich mystic: that's what I want to be.

❖

I broke my tongue on God.

❖

The true way is close, just as the remove from madness is close.

❖

Every man is in nirvana, if he but knows it.

❖

I *love* how a skeleton looks.

❖

I must learn that we must die.

❖

We have failed to live up to our geography.

❖

Every discovery makes its own chaos.

❖

A splendid day. Talked only to people.

❖

There'll be plenty of room in eternity for us all.

❖

The clock beat me again.

# THE POET'S BUSINESS

## (1943–47)

It's the poet's business to be more, not less, than a man.

✳

A poet: someone who is never satisfied with saying one thing at a time.

✳

Poetry: a sense of the doubleness in life.

✳

Poet: a constant selectivity; a refusal to elucidate with a mass of detail.

✳

A poet must be a good reporter; but he must be something a good deal more.

✳

Literalness is the devil's weapon.

✳

The eye, of course, is not enough. But the outer eye serves the inner, that's the point.

✳

One does not deny even a poetry of comment; little cadenced messages of uplift with the mild factitious strength of the hortatory. They come creeping out of the headlines. *Twiddlers:* so faithful to a negligible emotion . . .

✣

A moral sense can have other outlets than the rhymed sermon or editorial.

✣

The things that concern you most can't be put in prose. In prose the tendency is to avoid inner responsibility. Poetry is the discovery of the legend of one's youth.

✣

Basis of poetry is *sensation:* many poets today deny sensation, or some have no sensation: the cult of the torpid.

✣

Count ideas incidental in a poem.

✣

Make the language take really desperate jumps.

✣

Talent talks; genius does.

✣

Don't say: create.

✣

Society doesn't create the artists; the artists create society.

✣

For the artist tells us what life is possible.

✣

Art is our defense against hysteria and death.

✣

There are only two passions in art; there are only love and hate—with endless modifications.

❊

Not suddenly but slowly words are beginning to take on a new life. Part of the business of the young is to repudiate, which is to do a kind of hating.

❊

It is time for affirmations by someone other than ninnies and fools.

❊

Poems that praise God must create the belief that God also believes in the writer of the poem.

❊

God is one of the biggest bores in English poetry.

❊

Poem: one more triumph over chaos.

❊

Remember: our deepest perceptions are a waste if we have no sense of form.

❊

Puts his thought in motion—the poet.

❊

Movement: one of the hardest things a beginner (an honest one) has to learn is how to sustain the energy of a poem: in other words, the basic rhythm. He may have a variety of fresh subject matter, slick imagery, sharp epithets, but if he can't make the words move, he has nothing.

❊

Each word bumping along by itself.

❊

These bad-ear poets: their consonants knock one against the other; they mouth.

✳

Rhythm depends on expecting.

✳

A wrenching of rhythms, verbal snorting; tootling on the raucous tin-ear, mechanized fancies: his poems have movement, sometimes they slide away from the subject.

✳

There is a kind of poet who imposes unnecessary limitations and difficulties on the language: who bellows with his mouth full of butter.

✳

A small thing well done is better than the pretentious failure. If a thing fails rhythmically it's nothing.

✳

Rhythm: creates a pattern into which our mental faculties fall; this cycle of expectancy calls for surprises. The poet, at least the good poet, provides them.

✳

A musical ear is a gift from nature: but like all gifts it can be developed.

✳

My design in short poems: to create the situation and the mood as quickly as possible: etch it in and have done; but is that enough? No. There must be symbolical force, weight, or a gravity of tone.

✳

No tiny tinks of random flicks from the invisible.

✳

Honesty: the only tricks of the real artist are technical.

✤

The great difference between *doing* and explaining what is
being done. One can be a conscious artist, and still not have to
*explain*.

✤

You can't make poetry simply by avoiding clichés.

✤

Moments: beware the poetry of moments. Many of those moments are literary, remember. They have a past, a dreary past.

✤

Diction: one of the problems of diction, in certain kinds of
poems, is to get all the words within a certain *range* of feeling; all elemental, all household, etc., etc. Often a very good
figure from another level or range will jar.

✤

Dangers: Substituting words for thought.
          The sneer is easy to master, and usually the mark of
          the adolescent.
          Beware when you think you have found what you
          want.

✤

Description: the landscape's usually better for a *sign* of the
human. But don't lug him in like an ambulant cabbage.

✤

Assignment: find an odd form in Herbert or Hardy, and write
an exact imitation.

✤

Style: Break in on the reader sideways.
          Think with the wise, talk like the common man:
                    Give noun a full swat,
                    But adjective, not.

✣

Inspiration: the important thing in life is to have the right kind of frustration.

✣

On small poems: a thing may be small but it need not be a cameo; it may be a cinder in the shoe or the mind's eye or a pain in the neck.

✣

Poet must first control, then dominate his medium . . .

✣

Response to the image is not free, but controlled by the context. The incongruous response—a common fault.

✣

Embroidering a few metaphors on his pale convictions.

✣

Much to be learnt from bad poems.

✣

One thing that literature would be greatly the better for
Would be a more restricted employment by authors of simile
and metaphor.

✣

Almost all language is dead metaphor.

✣

The idea of poetry itself is a vast metaphor.

✣

Simple and profound: how little there is.

✣

By espousing the simple I do not deny the subtle. The gnomic rather than the sententious.

❧

Don't be afraid of the dramatic poem. There you don't have to "think" and you can stand one step away from your cozy little selves, on occasion.

❧

It is hard to be both plain and direct and not appear a fool to contemporaries fed on allusions, sybilline coziness, hints and shadows.

❧

Exactness is unfashionable; connotative sloppiness is in.

❧

To mean what you say—and that's more than mere sincerity.

❧

A poet is judged, in part, by the influences he resists.

❧

A "movement" is a dead fashion.

❧

To learn to suck out the *best* in a fashion.

❧

Many famous poems are simply landmarks of bad taste.

❧

Despite its effort to be surprising, so much of modern verse seems tensionless.
Sensory sharpness: lost in most.

❧

One of the subtlest tasks is the sifting from time. Some poems have that special sheen of contemporaneousness, the immediate glitter of fashion—and still survive.

❧

Degrees of comparison: pitches of suchness.

✳

Too eager to say what a lot of people will want to hear.

✳

False obliquity: the preconceived commonplace whipped into some shape.

✳

If the danger of the lover consists of his restricted point of view, that of the poet is his awareness of the abysses that divide one kind of perception from the others.

✳

A poet is a goof that doesn't have to bother to think—what the Man in the Street thinks.

✳

The young artist: there is no other kind of mind but my own.

✳

Continual writing is really a bad form of dissipation; it drains away the marrow of the brain.

✳

Perhaps no person can be a poet, or even can enjoy poetry, without a certain unsoundness of mind.

✳

What do we need to know? The history of ideas can get more evidence from the reading of poetry than vice versa. Same with source-chasing.

✳

This wanting a background, when one has the whole background of history, or fate, of time.

✳

The artist has several levels of life always available. If he falls to the ground with a theme or gets a "block," he can always return to life—to the routine task.

✻

Ability to revert to elementary beauties: a test that our judgments remain sound.

✻

His method of composition itself exemplified the material: the hunt for the clues to reality.

✻

There comes a time in the poet's life when one personality, even with several sides, is not enough. Then he can either go mad or become a dramatist.

✻

Freedom has its tyrannies—even in verse.

✻

When you begin to get good, you'll arouse the haters of life.

✻

We can love ourselves and literature with equal intensity—that's our contribution.

✻

A love of poetry that passes all understanding, indeed, that requires all understanding.

✻

I long to be a greater failure in life so I can write better books.

✻

How wonderful to write with a small pen: the recovery of precision.

✻

A poem that is the shape of the psyche itself; in times of great stress, that's what I tried to write.

❋

The sense that everything conspires against the poem: dark, light, dinner, defecation. My bones bleed from the harsh task.

❋

The poem that is merely painful revelations: my impulse is to tell you everything—which may destroy everything.

❋

Did I beat the poems to death? Did I worry the material like a mad dog?

❋

The poet: would rather eat a heart than a hambone.

❋

I am a poet: I am always hungry.

❋

There are so many ways of going to pot as a poet; so many pitfalls, so many snares and delusions.

❋

I used to think of poets as helping one another, as advancing consciousness together.

❋

"You try to tell us in short-hand; we don't even know long-hand." Swallow or strangle is my method.

❋

O the enormous folly of words.

❋

Move over, sensitive sad minds.

❋

Live in a perpetual great astonishment.

# WORDS FOR YOUNG WRITERS

## (1948–49)

Great teachers are not necessarily systematic thinkers. The very act of teaching is against this.

✻

For teaching is one of the central mysteries, in spite of its great body of unessential lore, its professors of silly procedure, the assemblers of material looser than newspapers . . .

✻

Today I'm going to lecture on confusion. I'm all for it.

✻

To find out something about your life: that will be the purpose. It may be necessary to change some of your ways of acting and thinking in this course. The burden will lie on you a good deal more; but it also, I wish you to understand, will lie on me a good deal more. It is much easier for me to lecture than it is for me to store up your various reactions, attitudes, keep turning them over in mind, letting my unconscious, my creative capacity evolve something, make a synthesis; come through with the right nudges, jeers, japes, kind or harsh words which will bring you into fuller being. Crudely put, it is like this: I'm willing to give you a chunk of myself—my time, my patience, my talent—*if* you want it.

The attempt is neither grandiose nor impertinent. I shall not try to poke and pry at your deepest self, or attempt to play the omniscient furious papa, the mentor, the great man —or any of those other odious roles which any teacher of energy can fall into so easily—and still, mind you, do much more for his students than those pitiful time-servers in the profession: the army of mediocrities, the indifferent, the lazy, the bored, the frightened or unsure who cover up their own grinding sense of inadequacy by the austere false front, or those contemptuous of the young—an even more dangerous type—often gifted. They forget, usually, that they themselves did not spring fully mature from the brow of Jove: they forget the vast patience of others who labored for them, often unbeknownst to them. Arrogance, in our profession, is an understandable sin, especially when one considers the brutalization, the crassness of much of contemporary life; the debased ethics of most of the professions; the dead pall that hangs over the spirit. But it is, nonetheless, a sin.

Faith. That's it. This course is an act of faith. In what? In the imagination of us all, in a creative capacity—that most sacred thing—that lies dormant, *never* dead, in everyone.

My amiability lasts only through the opening day. From now on, it's blood, sweat, and jeers. And suppose you do get good: get to the level of being able to publish in decent places, as a dozen or so have done. From then on it's even tougher . . . You must be fascinated, like Yeats, with the difficult. I'd like to see some of you have the absolutely dead-earnest seriousness, the naiveté, the love of poetry that prompted one gal at Bennington to come up and say, "Mr. Roethke, is there anything to this?" (handing over a poem).

Don't tell me over again what *I* say: already I'm tired of it. Build from it. I'm no swami, no guru, no Dr. Johnson, no high priest of poesy. And suppose you really *are* better than that. (Oh, I've had them, and even my toughest contemporaries have agreed.) Remember: "The world from earth to sky shows itself hostile to genius."

*

Moan somewhere else, text-creepers.

❋

There isn't time for good taste.

❋

We must have the courage, as Kierkegaard says, to think a thought whole.

❋

Solve all the leaps of light.

❋

The poet must have a sense not only of what words were and are, but also what they are going to be.

❋

Maybe, more age upon me, I'll care for the grave and ceremonious. But I doubt it.

❋

Poetry is not a mere shuffling of dead words or even a corralling of live ones.

❋

Say to yourself: I will learn and treasure every good turn of speech ever made.

❋

Plain speech is inaccurate but not plain words.

❋

In our age, if a boy or girl is untalented, the odds are in favor of their thinking they want to write.

❋

The intuitive poet often begins most felicitously, but raptures are hard to sustain.

❋

Transcend that vision. What is first or early is easy to believe. But . . . it may enchain you.

❖

I dream of a culture where it is thought a crime to be dull.

❖

Give me the madman's sudden insight and the child's spiritual dignity.

❖

Play with it—if you know what I don't mean. The language has its cusses and fusses just like us.

❖

Hopkins . . . didn't play enough: dear sweet serious man, so full, in spite of all his rigors, of that dangerous pride in his intellectual self. But how could he do it without the pride of an artist?

❖

The Victorians—they didn't let enough go in or go out. They lived in ponds.

❖

Tennyson lay down with the words of the day.

❖

Never be ashamed of the strange.

❖

Those who are willing to be vulnerable move among mysteries.

❖

There is an academic precept which says: never listen to the young. The reverse should be true: Listen, I say, and listen close, for from them—if they are real and alive—may we hear, however faintly and distortedly—the true whispers from the infinite, the beckonings away from the dreadful, the gray life beating itself against the pitted concrete world.

❖

Reject nothing, but re-order all.

❊

When were choices ever easy, analyst? You still read as if you were eating the page.

❊

There's nothing like ignorance to engender wild enthusiasm.

❊

One of those bright young men who spends all his time being right; a brisk metallic negative intelligence.

❊

They're almost too loyal to the context: those lyric poets constantly tuning themselves up for a note they never reach.

❊

The coarse sniggering behind that gruesome sentimentality.

❊

The literature of exasperation has few noble examples.

❊

A hatred for the way in which he works: so creeping, pistly, timorous, rank, and spiting.

❊

The voice-box is not a meat grinder . . .

❊

Observe, random energist, the bear's placidity.

❊

Some of these Limeys write as if they were falling over chairs.

❊

Love poems are written by the frustrated; religious poems often by the satiated.

❊

There should be a moratorium on all poems about music.

*

His ideas were few and very between.

*

Some vast and shabby uncle of disorder: an old dog barking in a cellar . . .

*

They've sat on the secret of life so long, they no longer realize it's there.

*

O dealer in momentous bromides, O odious ethereal chimney . . .

*

Their poems are not so much hewn as spewn.

*

The most bitter of intellectuals: he who was once a poet.

*

It's not that many Americans can't think: they just don't want to.

*

The delusion that there is some hidden mystery in the banal that escapes us.

*

The academic tendency to rest: that profound impulse to sit down.

*

What we need is more people who specialize in the impossible.

*

O the lies I have told to my own energies!

✤

The serious problems of life are never fully solved but some
states can be resolved rhythmically.

✤

The decasyllabic line is fine for someone who wants to meditate
—or maunder. Me, I need something to jump in: hence the
spins and shifts, the songs, the rants and howls. The shorter
line can still serve us: it did when English was young, and
when we were children.

✤

There are those who can hold forth, but me, I have to holler.

✤

Can't we shake things up enough so a high, intense, passionate
speech will be heard? When a long soliloquy will be listened to
without trick stage effects or Pretty Sir Somebody's posterior in
velveteen pants?

✤

To make it so good that there will be no actors will ever act it
right: but none can be so bad, in any windy barn, to foul it up
entirely.

✤

There are only a few bony concepts, but think of the metaphors!

✤

The resonant, the orotund, the rounding of
The round full phrases sounding like far sighs,
As if an ancient hill has found a motion
Long remembered, never brought to action . . .

✤

The tragedy inherent in enhancing tradition: to embrace the
dead in the right way; or how to kiss a ghost.

*

Haven't all the ways of being formal and fancy, for this moment in time, been mastered? Even Yeats in his high speech grates on me much of the time. How grateful I am to forget them, those contemporaries whom one honors by doing otherwise! Stevens to the left of me, Cummings to the right of me—goodbye, Louise and Rolfe, this silly's escaping into his own life at last.

*

Full of slang, japes, stale jokes, but lively and funny, and sad at times, with the sadness of animals, moping bears and other things that live by and below the nose . . . O keep me perpetual, muse, ears roaring with many things . . .

*

Get down where your obsessions are. For Christ's sake, shake it loose. Make like a dream, but not a dreamy poem. The past is asking. You can't go dibble dabble in your tears. The fungi will come running; the mould will begin all over the noble lineaments of the soul. Remember: a fake compassion covers up many a sore. Keep more than your nose clean. Abstinence makes the heart meander. Even the vapors are twitching. Certainly, flesh, I hear you perfectly. But this time and place is for something else.
Sit here, the rocks are warm, sing the sirens,
Listen to them and your belly will soon be a pudding.
Instead, prance with the cats,
See what the soft woods say,
Let the nerves sing, and the soul, for the time being, keep silent.
The eyes have it. Remember: the dead keep out the half-dead—
Those dreary language-arrangers. Don't be ashamed if you belch when you try to sing. You may be a visceral spinner . . .

✤

The evocative may be the cry of life itself—but what a grotesque form it takes!

✤

These words I have dredged: they have all the charm of aborted salamanders, an old turtle full of bloodsuckers and sores.

✤

May my silences become more accurate.

✤

Words wear me away.

✤

And every day I curse my bad education . . .

✤

There's an element of desperation in the insistence of the graduate student's respect for knowledge—as opposed to wisdom.

✤

There is no end to what should be known about words.

✤

I can't die just now. There's too much to do.

✤

Here's to that old harpy who slips me a few sips of the sacred juice, as well as an occasional Mickey Finn.

✤

I know nothing you have not forgotten, young as you are.

✤

The wisdom the young make holy by their living: so intense, yet thin, the weedy pierce of pleasure, as a bush bends yet replies, riding the stream of air always around it.

✳

The true verbal surprise: the unreal is actually the beginning.
It is what we want in the young poet: the fresh metaphor.

✳

It's hard to get at 'em. You think you've split the heart of
reality—for a moment or two, maybe—and there they are, still
bland and decorous.

✳

We're not going to split the heart of reality: not until the third
semester.

✳

Why should discussions disappear, the edge of thought slide so
far away, the shade of what we said be less, be less . . .
Thought changes into the shade of light.

✳

Hearing poetry starts the psychological mechanism of prayer.

✳

The only thing I want to write about is light, what's in the eye
and the stone.

✳

The words grappling across my tongue, things never said coming across the lip's threshold . . .

✳

It's your privilege to find me incomprehensible. I gave you my
minutes; let them remain ours. I hope I haunt you. Goodbye,
swan-shapes, dear turtles, witches. An aging man can't tell you
a thing. This is only a rage of fat.

✳

He teaches a class like an animal trainer.

✳

The cage is open: you may go.

# THE PROVERBS OF PURGATORY

(1948–49)

All time hangs on a nail.

✻

Hatred of life can rise to a mystical state.

✻

For him, God was always there, like an ugly wife.

✻

Despair and the most transcendental love of God are inseparable.

✻

Arrogance and boredom are the two most authentic products of hell.

✻

The weapons of the weak are too violent.

✻

All interiors call.

✻

The directionless learn only by moving.

✻

Those who almost see are the most terrified.

✻

In a house of louts, I lived much too happy.

✻

I eat what I believe.

＊

As for spiritual brashness—there are worse qualities.

＊

Live with the desperate and you'll survive those moderate fears.

＊

Surround yourself with rising waters: the flood will teach you to swim.

＊

Sex and death: the two things you must use and not abuse, my children.

＊

He that lives by the skin will die in it.

＊

The Devil is intuitive, not articulate . . .

＊

Oh, some forms of aggression are lovely!

＊

The passive are first bewildered, then malicious.

＊

More than two days in Detroit is not permitted the human psyche.

＊

The Devil today takes the form of noise.

＊

God does not like to be asked too violently to step in.

＊

If you can't keep up, go back.

✣

Only the disciplined can know the profound magnificence of this disorder.

✣

Vision is the end of religion.

✣

I am; therefore, I continue.

✣

Time marks us while we're marking time.

✣

Dreaming, we awake the dead.

✣

The curious eat themselves.

✣

The angels ask but never answer.

✣

Even a fire kisses itself.

# I TEACH OUT OF LOVE

## (1949–53)

English teaching, in one sense, is dreadful just insofar as it is a profession.

✻

One of the principal techniques of teaching is the barrage of half-truths, the throwing-up of ideas to be resisted, to be discarded, eventually. Good as it is pedagogically, it can affect, possibly to the point of damage, what the user of such a method holds forth publicly. His thoughts inevitably will have the accent of the careless improvisation: the mock belligerence of the man who hopes to be answered, corrected, or denied.

✻

One teaches out of love: it's an impertinence, an imposition, in the end it's terrifying.

✻

When I say I teach out of love, I mean just that, by God.

✻

The young are often impressed with a mindless vehemence. They may be right.

✻

All essays should be, not trials, but celebrations.

✻

The nobility of the imagination is my theme: I have to let things shimmer.

❋

My strength is the strength
Of ten young things: I am with you:
In that first moment of delight
When you look from the page, no longer lost
In the maze of your youth . . .

❋

Virtue and poetry cannot be taught: they presuppose a genuine
desire to make something, a love, an ear for, the language.

❋

What's your business? Waking the wits of bitches.

❋

The most difficult thing to remember: that a poem is made
of words.

❋

Your words are you. You are *them* and not much more.
The Description: the fieldness of fields, the weediness of
weeds . . . When is description mere? Never. A freshness
in the seeing, an innocency in the vision, the angle of perception, the bringing together of details, not necessarily as
metaphors, even, just as objects. Be one of those on whom,
as Lawrence said, nothing is lost. Don't strain for arrangement.
Look and put it down and let your sensibility be the sieve.

❋

We must escape from the well-made poem and find ourselves
in the material all over again. Don't grovel before words. My
task is not to woo you into being.

❋

The splendid irrationality of a peacock's tail.

✣

I teach nothing but the obvious. But that's nearly always forgotten.

✣

That's the horrible thing about being a genius. Everything's
so obvious.

✣

The story seems to be that I am some sort of swami who
can stare deep deep into coed eyes and pluck forth some
liquid shimmering truth, neat as a fish . . .

✣

I'll teach you all I've forgotten.

✣

Not to arrange little pieces of factitious feeling.

✣

Something gay and tumultuous, in a yeasty rare high contumely.

✣

Poetry is an act of mischief.

✣

The poem of the immediate situation: that attempts to give
the reader the sense of being right in the banal: the problem
is tougher in poetry than in fiction (Auden's sonnet on the
novelist who suffers dully). The poem should provide that
break, that vision into reality which relieves and makes alive.

✣

The essence of prose is to perish—that is to say, to be "under-
stood."

✣

Realism is no longer possible: for that world has been drained
and scoured to gray by the formaldehyde of reportage.

✷

The violent effort to break from what is around him in the modern poet: not so much to startle the reader as to startle himself.

✷

It is well to keep in touch with chaos.

✷

Exaggeration: a lovely thing but it must come naturally . . .

✷

Not a spoken—in the sense of cadenced—speech, however grave and beautiful that has been on some lips and still can be; but we need a speech so flexible, so plastic, we're alive to every nuance that the language has . . .

✷

Language as complicated as James' and yet passionate, full of auditory shocks and shifts . . .

✷

The lyric is almost forgotten in this time of sawing and snoring and scraping.

✷

A poet's rhythmical energy is, I should say, the index to his psychic energy  . .

✷

In the purely verbal medium if the condition of music is approached too closely, then tenuousness or (if the personality of the writer is strong) chaos ensues.

✷

There is much to be learned and wrung from terror, anxiety, fear: there are still "forms" which the imagination can seize from these dark seas of the mind and spirit.

✵

Pardon me, Apple.
Hello, Worm.
Here's the Secret
Of Pure Form.

✵

Art is the means we have of undoing the damage of haste.
It's what everything else isn't.

✵

A poetry of longing: not for escape, but for a greater reality.

✵

I'd say the intuitive worker might take some hints from what
Yeats did at the very last in "High Talk" . . .

✵

So many writers are an immense diasppointment: they're
neurotic, grubby, cozy, frightened, eaten by their wits . . .

✵

The poet is reduced, psychologically, to being either an ironical
mouse or a bar-room blow-hard.

✵

These may be matters only a fool or a saint should mention.
I am neither. And I carry no more great charity or regard
for most immediate contemporaries than the late W. C. Fields;
the usual I-can-write-better-with-chalk-in-my-navel reaction.

✵

I have said uncharitable things even in sleep about every new
critic that ever wrote.

✵

Those louts, let them starve with their coarse abstractions,
Let them wither away on their blighted trees,
Dying like dead crows tied to broom-sticks . . .

✤

Those poets who go around as if they had just committed a nuisance.

✤

They write premonitory poetry after the changes have arrived.

✤

Lawrence: there are other kinds of immediacy: so on top of life, he smothered it.

✤

A new-bathed man approaching a smell: Eliot toward much of his material.

✤

English poetry: mostly by ninnies, capable of fits and starts of ravishing feeling—Peele, for instance—but scarcely capable of filling out a simple tax form.

✤

This one ate his father; this one saves his grandmother's toe-nails;
This one bites his nails; this one is master of the slack line;
This one cries in the dark; this one faints in a paroxysm of understatement.

✤

Exasperation is one of the means we have of reminding ourselves that most people are—not dead—but in a milky state of inanition: a diet-milk the color of putty.

✤

Not the stuff, but merely the stuffing, of real poetry. An anthology of abstractions from one of the less sure metaphysicians: a nowadays nausea.

✤

That editor who bemoans the passing of what he has spent his life trying to kill: the full free effect.

✤

All the charm of a doorknob in a public toilet.

✤

These fancy dandlers of mild epithets, graceless wittols hanging on the coattails of their betters. I can forget what they do until they forget to steal and start being themselves . . .

✤

They make out by the sheer weight, the momentum of their tastelessness.

✤

He had all the charity of a cruising shark.

✤

He was the master of the remark that insults everybody— including himself.

✤

Even a bad piece of writing can have its own mysterious life, and be a fascination.

✤

Isn't there something else? Must we have nothing but this leaping and snorting in the dark, these whimsey-itches, small-fry frenzies, silent-night sweatings, yippety-yap yodellings? Why not a dull one-legged dour poem?

✤

The doubleness of all things has oppressed me. Gayety and nonchalance: in verse, in life so rare.

❋

The fallacious doctrine that all that is good in writing *must* come at a heavy, even a tragic, cost. We distrust the vicarious experience or do not have faith in the powers of the imagination. Such unimpeachable joys assail me!

❋

In my poems, there is much more reality than in any relationship or affection that I feel; when I create, I am true, and I would like to find the strength to base my life entirely on this truth, on this infinite simplicity and joy . . .

❋

I work very slowly: I can afford to be terribly spontaneous.

❋

I was a man committed to the concrete.

❋

I need the botanist's leaf more than the poet's flower.

❋

Is associational thinking just a trick? If so, it's a good one, and for some of the slow boys, of whom I am one, it takes very long to learn.

❋

When I think of the time Rilke had, I could weep: and the things about him which tied him to the past and helped make him human.

❋

This Caliban of the classroom, old Uncle Hot Poop, a bug-eyed blubbering boy—his burden's made him nervous but he can't relieve himself. Allow me, dear pussies, just a few more evocative squawks.

❋

You didn't want to learn everything, and, by God, you haven't.

❋

It takes so much time to be fair.

❋

Maturity in a poet: when he no longer is concerned with personal mortality . . . but whether the language dies.

❋

What we forget is the effect we have on the young: that we are their lives in a way that is no longer quite realizable to us.

❋

Here it is: all signs, semblances, analogies: all teeming, teaming with life and love.

❋

Now what's the way to proceed? To snow the future with poems, indulge in every poetic fancy that comes into your heads, or *provide release*—and leave the burden of sifting out the over-peculiar, the wild exaggerations to others?

❋

Go thou and do otherwise.

❋

When he ran out of material, Yeats invented himself.

❋

Eternal apprenticeship is the life of the true poet.

❋

We are condemned to singing when we can;
Each long root blossoms to a different sun.

❋

The only wisdom he acquired was from poetry: a special wisdom of feeling, not a refinement of feeling.

❋

I'm crying for what I can never do.

✣

Mother of God, I just invented a few sayings out of me head.
Is that wicked?

✣

That intense desire to go back to teach them more, to stay
with their lives, to have their faces and limbs as I had them . . .

✣

My words are not with you:
I'm only an old tune
Dying on a stone.
You'll remember me
Alone and clucking in the cold,
A mother-hen hatching out some supreme wickedness,
Writhing and seething under layers of wool and linen.
By a voice back of the moon, you will be reminded,
With the deep stream, you will remember:
And I, perhaps alive in a phrase,
Will manage, I think, a laugh
From under the weight of my beard and the mouldering stones.

# FIRST CLASS

## (1950–53)

Stick out your can, here comes a lesson-plan.

✤

Flat words from a fat boy. What pearls are there to cast to colleagues?

✤

To teach by suggestion or "intuitively" takes more time than teaching by precept or lecturing. For you carry the students in your mind and in reading think, "There's a swell example to show Flossie. . . ." To teach very fast, by associational jumps—to teach a class as a *poem*—is dangerous but very exciting. It is possible to build up a "charge" with a group and blast away in a kind of mass diagnosis.

✤

I used to teach like killing snakes: a constant pressuring.

✤

To teach too intensively is to get so involved in particular psyches that there can be an actual loss of identity; destructive both to student and teacher. I remember a student saying, "You carry us farther than we could ever go alone. Then when you're gone, it's too much to face." Let's face it: much of this kind of teaching may perform the function of psychiatry, but it is absolutely fatal to proceed from such a premise or become self-conscious about what you're up to.

✤

My teaching is a variety of coaching, really: both athletic and musical.

❊

Most good teachers attempt the Socratic assumption of ignorance, but are often handicapped by their very real and sometimes vast knowledge: I have the advantage over such fellows in that I really don't know anything and can function purely: the students *have* to teach themselves.

❊

If you teach by suggestion, there must be plenty to suggest from—a bale of examples. Anthologies are often inert.

❊

You're referee, and sometimes the job is as hazardous as in ice hockey. Sure, it's possible, with a tweed jacket and a pipe and a choice collection of polysyllables to hold certain of the young at bay, to cow them. But they won't be the best ones.

❊

We expect the hot flash and we get the cold stale inert lumpish inanities, the heavy archness, the smirking self-satisfaction.

❊

Are there dangers? Of course. There are dangers every time I open my mouth, hence at times when I keep it shut, I try to teach by grunts, sighs, shrugs.

❊

To the extent that I talk, I am a failure as a teacher.

❊

You can't go out to all of them: all the way. That way lies madness and death. As it is, you work harder than most psychiatrists—and get much further faster, more humanly, painlessly.

❊

I ask you: I beg you: bring to this task all the sweetness of spirit you possesss. Leave your neuroses at home, and while there, make them work for you, or exorcise them from your best being.

✶

A too excessive concern over students can mean: 1) death of the teacher; 2) distortion of the student: a sense of weakness or reliance.

✶

The essential thing: that they not be loused up, warped, unduly twisted, played upon, brought to the wrong ends, led to the stony pasture.

✶

I'd rather just sit around and dribble little bits of teaching wisdom . . . one of the more valiantly disorganized minds of our time.

✶

In teaching, gruffness may be the true *cortesia*.

✶

In writing you must go ahead; in teaching, so much of the time, you must go back.

✶

I take it I'm to stand up for Poesy, but not say anything to make anyone nervous. For you know: one of the problems of the lyric poet is what to do with his spare time; and sometimes it becomes the community's problem too. It worries people. I know when I came out to Seattle, the head of my department said, "Ted, we don't know quite what to do with you: you're the only serious practicing poet within 1500 miles." I sort of was given to understand I had a status between—if it were Oklahoma—between a bank-robber and a Congressman.

✶

Teaching: one of the few professions that permit love.

*

Look, I'm the greatest dumb teacher alive.

*

You think and I'll say.

*

Look how "wicked" we are: we have a poet who's a full professor.

*

A hot shot of the hard word—is that what you want? I feel strangely diffident. I'm a sport, an anachronism: nobody ever told me where to go.

*

I've had a most savage attack of humility of late; the notion that seems to horrify some of you is that you're not only expected to do some work, but actually supposed to teach the teacher. I assure you that this is astonishingly easy to do.

*

How wonderful the struggle with language is.

*

The recording apparatus must be mature: complete and steady enough to rely on itself. There can't be any brash barkings into the bass drum or simpers off into the wings or cozy thigh-crossings: everybody hates the unformed. You're a speaking foetus, get it? A soft-boiled egg wobbling on one leg, looking for the edge of a cup or saucer . . . You roar, not from a true disquietude of the heart, but from growing-pains . . . spiritual teething. This fledgling's cheep would disgrace a magpie.

*

When you roar, make sure it's from a true disquietude of the heart, not a mere temporal pinch . . . In the end, if you aspire to the visionary's toughness, you not only have to chew your own marrow, but then must spit it in your neighbor's eye.

✻

In this first assignment just care about words. Dwell on them lovingly.

✻

For Christ's sake, awake and sing! You're as conditioned as old sheep.

✻

It's the damned almost-language that's hardest to break away from: the skilled words of the literary poet.

✻

The artist (not the would-be): you may have deep insights— but you also need the sense of form. Sometimes the possession of the first without the second may be tragic.

✻

Good poets wait for the muse, the unconscious to spring something loose, to temper and test the promptings of the intuition with the pressures of craftsmanship: they can think while they sing.

✻

If only this rare rich ripe deviousness could be put to some useful work.

✻

I'll deliver you, dear doves, out of the rational, into the realm of pure song.

✻

It's true many of the lessons are the same; in fact, almost reduce themselves to one lesson: cutting. But the applications, the variations are infinite.

❋

To be too explicit destroys the pleasure. This the Irish know, to whom the half-said's dearest.

❋

I have to be concrete. Everything else scares the hell out of me.

❋

Immobility is fatal in the arts.

❋

To bring you out of that purposelessness—surely that is a great thing, even if you move but an inch from yourselves . . .

❋

The artist doesn't want to be articulate about something until he is finally articulate. One can talk away certain themes, spoil them.

❋

That intense profound sharp longing to make a true poem.

❋

One form of the death wish is the embracing of mediocrity: a deliberate reading and re-reading of newspapers . . .

❋

Today there's no time for the mistakes of a long and slow development: dazzle or die. Would Yeats' career be possible in this country today?

❋

The "other" poems in Yeats . . . had to set the stage for his best work. If he had not written at such length, he might not have been heard.

❋

What would you rather be—happy or Hölderlin?

❖

Much of poetry is an anguished waiting.

❖

One of the virtues of good poetry is the fact that it irritates the mediocre.

❖

I can't understand the condescension many "professional" poets have for the young. Usually it seems defensive, a form of fear or even a kind of jealousy.

❖

Uncle Easy,
You mustn't be queasy:
I haven't forgotten
Cousin Rotten.

❖

Behold the heavy-footed bard
With rhythms from the lumberyard.

❖

In him all the oafs, dolts, bumpkins, and clods, living and dead, connect and contend.

❖

A bewildered bardling: no real feeling except a thin intense hatred of his contemporary superiors.

❖

The gusty, self-appreciating tone
Is something only he can make his own:
The true provincial wit, he never reads
Except the thing his little spirit needs:
I find it comic that he speaks of *voice*
Who never made a rhythm without noise.

✤

A great one for hurrahing early work; but as soon as the subject departs from the rude thumps and lubberly staves of the lisping idiot boy, he has "abandoned his muse" or is depending on mere cleverness. What a burden he bears, carrying the weight of criticism for us all. How fiercely he guards his few nuggets of wisdom. In the perpetual hunt for merit, he is content to scavenge.

✤

The critics: they have taught poets much about what not to do—for one thing, to avoid pleasing them.

✤

The critic's attitude: this poem exists for me to verbalize about it.

✤

A culture in which it is easier to publish a book about poetry than a book of poems.

✤

These shabby detractors; these cheap cavillers, gurgling with their jargon: they're fatter in the head than the worst priests of disillusion.

✤

The pip-squeak peripheral dippers: they could come to a full circle in the middle of a plugged nickel: it's no good declaring them frauds: they retain their dubious virtues. It's true in the tiny areas they leak and squeak in: sand-fleas of the soul on the immense beaches of desolation. Meanwhile the wind's where it is: the sun plays in the dark leaves of the acanthus. Locality is alive . . .

✤

How do I know what I said? Half the time I wasn't listening.

❋

I was committed to the future: and in a sense only the future existed.

❋

I don't think anybody ever yearned more for a public than I did.

❋

What have I done, dear God, to deserve this perpetual feeling that I'm almost ready to begin something really new?

❋

A profound dissatisfaction with these tin-cans, frigidaires, barbered prose, milk and water fantasies.

❋

If poetry can kill you, I'm like to die.

❋

The exactly right goose to a tired psyche: the Socratic method is exhausting with uneven material; worse with limited. To hell, I say, with the conference. It's enough for me to listen, and cut away, and suggest, quickly. Come up before or after class. None of this breast-feeding.

❋

Well, well, have I become no more a dug? Let's have an end to this shameless breast-feeding from one who doesn't pretend to know anyway: you don't cut the mustard always with silver: Any old stick, pie-tin, or pencil's material to beat out the meter of happy bones.

❋

We may not be going far: but even beyond the door is a great way in this journey. "I've lost it," he said: the gift for the creative reverie. I no longer listen and wait, but hear only the snapping clichés, our whole life driving toward coarse abstractions.

A honey-seeker numb as a bee in November.
To recover the fine extravagance, the bravado, the true
bravura . . .
To find my own labyrinth and wind there,
A placid worm . . .
You two trees, don't think you're a wood . . .
My feet leap with the dancing dead . . .
What to do when the fresh metaphors flash forth—that is a
facer . . .
For who would tinker when the muses say?
I call the light out of someone else.
Sing up, sing all, a Socrates of fury.

# THE RIGHT TO SAY MAYBE

## (1948–53)

I provide the chaos: you the chronos.

✻

Today, or tonight, I realized finally at the age of 40, for the first time, that it is really possible for me to think, and even get pleasure from the process. Not that my efforts—or effects—are spectacular. Perhaps four consecutive related thoughts at present is the absolute top of my form—and that only just before falling asleep, or just after eating a fine breakfast, when I'm too lazy to write anything down. But still, even this is a beginning. And such excitement!

✻

Definition of a philosopher: a man who has the right to say maybe.

✻

Tonight I looked at Wilfred's (the cat's) mouth and was struck by its beauty. An inexpressible feeling of tenderness for it . . .

✻

In moments of tense depression, natural things, particularly fences, appear more beautiful—heart-breakingly so.

✻

Me, if I'm depressed, I go down to the A & P and admire the lemons and bananas, the meat and milk.

✻

I remember telling Kenneth Burke that I was saving for my old age two things: the belief in God and a consideration of abstract thought. Both are beginning, and there's no alas in me.

❊

A man who knows what his hallucinations mean and acts upon them; who in his most desperate time snatches some wisdom from the fire . . .

❊

I know where the half-dead hug their last secrets: the fungi-focus, inertia's children; how they stay there—limp as drenched insects—so happy with themselves.

❊

You're a living example that the mystics were right: we *must* escape the ego.

❊

He'd turn the light off on a moth.

❊

I notice even Schweitzer lashes out against mediocrity, especially when it weakens the good.

❊

In spite of all the paraphernalia for keeping things together, how haphazard life is, and the judgments of time.

❊

An age can be judged by the quality of its failures.

❊

Surely goodness and mercy can be more choosy.

❊

The spiritual growth's an oscillatory thing: we move by shivers in the world's tumultuous spine.

❊

Time goes up and down; but I go back and forth.

❊

The terrifying spectacle of young blood carrying out the missions of hypocrisy, ready to die for what no one cares about . . .

*

The coarse hunger of a raw soul: a fish loose in the grass, slopping and slipping.

*

O haters of life, how you are hated! And I defile myself with this fury.

*

A time when only the mad know the extravagances of love.

*

I have begun, again, my long training as an enemy of contemporary custom.

*

The death of feeling in a child: what is more terrible?

*

Alas, he's degenerated into a civilized man.

*

He hasn't got room in his life for a dog or a cat. All he's got room for is improvement.

*

It takes a heap of living in a whom to make it whom.

*

As usual, there's more garbage than cans.

*

To be less than you are is so easy: even a child needs no lessons in this.

*

The suicide's thought: at least *this* will be done.

*

Civilization is overrated: but there isn't anything much else.

❉

We have come to expect the public man, at best, to be third-rate; most of the time. A considerable section of influential American public men are simply hillbillies who have learned to count.

❉

Wisdom increases and is a burden. I know too many people and why I should love them, and the thought that I love them imperfectly is a constant vexation. My half-life continues. The great error of the American condition: to forget that people are humanity—I don't mean in the cliché sense—but are a part of the whole stream of history, and, whatever else they may be in the Here and Now, should be respected and considered, and loved as far as possible and not thought of as students, colleagues, anonymous neighbors.

❉

To be all things to all men—that's the saint's job—and, with all my sins on me, I attempt it. It's enough to make stronger men than me mad.

❉

I wish I had the energy to love you all.

❉

Why? I don't understand it. Hatred? I really don't, though it's part of me. And the sad lack is that even hating hatred's a hate that kills something . . .

❉

Common sense: the insight of mediocrity.

❉

I pray for the death of common sense.

❉

The longer I live, the tireder I get of good taste.

✣

Having fought through, perhaps for years, to understand an experience, and having at last come to that experience, how quick we are to resent someone else's not understanding it . . .

✣

For wisdom's reaches are so narrow still
That we may beat but cannot teach the will.

✣

I wish I could find an event that meant as much as simple seeing!

✣

There are few people who have had a more sincere hatred of thinking.

✣

With age, the pleasures of looking become more intense.

✣

The recovery of things is our business: See! we're blessed by what we see!

✣

History, for all its apparatus, appears to us primarily as a form of intuition.

✣

To each his own labyrinth.

✣

The first sense of the abyss: reason thrown back on itself.

✣

Each man creeps to his dark . . . The thin scratching on the walls of eternity.

✣

Only the young can save us. Most men—but not all—deteriorate.

✤

The young shall save us, and the noble rage.

✤

There are many terrifying kinds of stupidity, but that which disguises itself as skepticism is one that shudders me the most.

✤

Some of God's deals are rather coarse if we believe the mystics: "Think on me, and I will think on thee."

✤

The sense of sin must die.

✤

You who study the mystics have a curious lack of humility before life, before the creative. You should not let the adrenalin flush your brains.

✤

I look and find no wisdom anywhere.

✤

I'm sure God is bored with organized religion.

✤

I have no creed: my temper is devout.

✤

Those damned old mystics have got me despising myself.

✤

The great cause of God in us—where has it gone?

✤

I'm tired of human considerations. Let's have some inhuman considerations.

✤

God has even more trouble than we do.

❋

If God does not exist, neither do we.

❋

God, alone, is poor.

❋

God can't be a benign cozy foxy grandpa all the time: he gets mad too.

❋

Why are we "far" from God? Because he's more exasperated even than the best of us are with the state of things. And perhaps bored—particularly with our lack of resilience: our clumsy efforts . . .

❋

I don't give a damn about the eye of God; I can get along with it. It's the eyes of my neighbor that bother me.

❋

I always wanted to step in and out of reality; and after a while God let me.

❋

God is all which is *not me*.

❋

This separateness, once perceived, is a full look into the foul face of the infinite.

❋

I add—He takes away.
I remember—He concludes.
I despise—He can praise.

❋

God save my tongue. I'm creeping to the news.

❊

My God! Everything's breaking into principles! And here I've been parsing and parcelling myself!

❊

Self-knowledge: the supreme, perhaps the only, good?

❊

I demand from you, deepest self, some jaunty principle of order.

❊

He gave his mirror a look of great understanding.

❊

To be more than man: that German desire, that is my curse.

❊

The interior man buries the exterior.

❊

Make me evil or good, but make me something!

❊

I blush in a limited area.

❊

To stand on the edge of achievement: that is one of the more horrible of all states: an uncertain egg about to roll off the wall.

❊

To sit in the center of a blast; that's easier than wavering on the edges of a nightmare.

❊

Taking a hot seat in the heart of a lotus . . .

❊

Why is the evocative so powerfully attractive? It is more than a sign of weakness: it is a kind of universal recognition of our loss. Our loss as what? As humans, having come from some-where else.

❋

Not just a dedication, a focus of energies, but a desperateness to reach out to where I should be.

❋

The soul must suffer its own disintegration, unconsciously, if it is to survive.

❋

Like an old man, I stared between my hands.

❋

My lacks love me.

❋

I'm here, where time stares.

❋

Words hold me in: I'm alone with what I never said.

❋

These are my concordants: those contraries, happy never to meet.

❋

I can't fly—except into the wind.

❋

I'd live among the fish if I could.

❋

God, give me, not grace, but just energy enough to move around!

❋

I'm firing my feet of clay.

✢

Make me unworthy of my time. I'm famished by what others eat.

✢

In dreams begin responsibilities? The hell. In dreams the death-wish renews itself.

✢

I live in a half-night, outside a dream, yet not within life. My dreams don't understand me.

✢

Let me recover one least bit of my own mysteriousness! I'm all wiped and tidied: my ears can't hear what I've forgotten to say. And dear Aunt Anxiety has called twice before lunch.

✢

He's here, I said: whom you will never encompass, whom you will never understand.

✢

The apathy after terror is a kind of prelude, a flash into the horrors of old age.

✢

Suppose it should be that we break with joy just before we go down? Isn't that enough?

✢

Each day I'm less for death.

✢

Death shall not define me.

✢

This heart burst with its buried life.

✢

Both inner and outer reality the same: the final secret . . .

✤

Ah, was there ever a man who couldn't explain everything that ever was in terms of himself?

✤

May the hand of God wipe the blood from his brain.

✤

I am about the business of the dead.

✤

Earthling, the dark is true; the sun's an accident.

✤

All visions are of death.

✤

The vision of the world as dancing people: my God, that *is* the world to come.

✤

Water for meditation; stones for clamor;
Grass for beguilement; let our feet have peace . . .

✤

This is the whole eternity I know:
True dancers shall foregather . . .

✤

May your feet imitate heaven.

✤

Dust shall be, shall see.

✤

I believe, even in sleep.

# THE HAMMER'S KNOWLEDGE

---

(1954–58)

Truth, like God, is known only by manifestations.

*

Unless I've seen it, I don't know.

*

Only in language can the spirit yearn with dignity.

*

The ladder's privilege is the hammer's knowledge.

*

Will's a heady master: don't follow.

*

Ambition's a species of madness.

*

No man can sigh himself into eternity.

*

First intuition is of the unique, living self; the second is of the unique, dying self.

*

Death's image has a daily resurrection.

*

The vague is more dangerous than the arid.

*

Thoughts to be forgotten: the infinite rubbish of other men's inchoate experience.

*

Life is an offensive directed against the repetitive mechanism of the universe.

*

True freedom: being subject only to the eternal truth of things, not their appearances. Own nothing, owe everything.

*

We are predestined by what we have done with our free-will.

*

Evil: good in the wrong place.

*

Good does no good, and evil does no evil . . .

*

How weak the longing for the infinite among the sanctimonious.

*

The great mystery of Christianity is how it has lasted so long.

*

God is good: the supreme nonsense.

*

If we think long enough about God, we may create Him.

*

Does God *want* all that attention?

*

We can forgive others everything but our own weaknesses.

*

All knowledge lives in paradox.

*

It's even harder to be nice and bright than to be good and rich.

❊

Listen to the haters: they may remind you of new ways to love.

❊

Flesh pays for the soul's daring . . .

❊

Quiet is the complement of the moral state of humility.

❊

We bear this life by being, being bare.

❊

The spirit knows the body: head to toe.

❊

The body is the soul.

❊

I trust all joy.

# FROM ROETHKE TO GOETHE

## (1954–58)

From Roethke to Goethe isn't really so far:
Put a Capital G in for capital R—
Then knock out small k, a quite simple thing—
And you've got a fat cat fixed up like a king.

✳

Genius appears in strange places. Oddly enough, it has appeared in the form of me.

✳

We all long to create a great dreary masterpiece that everyone will have to pretend to read.

✳

The barrenness of the poetic task: as if every day we look out at a courtyard of rubble and from this are required to make something beautiful.

✳

"To ask the hard question is simple . . ."? (*Auden*) The hell it is. The true questions take a lifetime to find, to comprehend. The child's "What is God?" is light-years from the old angry poet's refusal to faint before the Cross.

✳

I can become a bird but I can't write a story.

✳

The artist needs, apparently, at least some appreciation of his work before he can effect the act of love.

✤

I've learned a lot from women, particularly women who thought I should be left under a stone.

✤

My racial memory includes all pretty women.

✤

Any virgin beyond 2 carries a certain authority.

✤

What's all my love for? Have I trained my feelings, refined my fingers only to be a fool?

✤

The act of poetry remains, for me, more mysterious than sex itself.

✤

There is a final triumph in the writing of a poem that goes beyond anything I understand.

✤

The provincial's danger is to love excessively—and irrationally.

✤

I think no one has ever spoken upon the peculiar, the absolute —can I say—cultural loneliness of the American provincial creative intellectual. I don't mention this as something to be sighed over, worried about, written about—simply say it is simple fact that the American is alone in space and time—history is not with him, he has no one to talk to— Well, the British do.

✤

I think often: all educated Englishmen are brighter than I am —but always worse artists.

✤

It may be, in these long pieces, I have seized and defiled certain types of rare experience.

✤

A clown quince of chi-chi, a daft babbler of daring obscenities, an oracular monster of sensibility. In other words, stop reading *my* longer poems as if they were something to emulate technically. They came out of a special and terrifying experience: I took chances on my life to write them, and I was a fool for doing so.

✤

Look, I'm not neurotic: or making this up or inducing these symbols. These things happen to a human body.

✤

I believe in presenting the material nakedly, dramatically: the language must be in me.

✤

I'm a terribly spontaneous writer: it takes me months, often, to get some of these tiny effects.

✤

There's always that next turn to what is really good, and I want to make that turn.

✤

As if I'm being tortured by the gods—this feeling there is some great task just beyond, a new triumphant rhythm.

✤

Dear God, don't make me intelligible . . . I'm to be known slowly.

✤

There are those who feel that a poetry reading should take on the nature of high mass: the utter, the absolute, dead silence, the dimming of lights, the sudden drawing back of the flap curtain, and there the poet under a single spot, stark naked. But personally I feel that the Catholics and the Episcopalians do it better—and why compete?

✤

I'm depressed. I wish I liked Henry James.

✤

My search for great men, even able men, grows longer and
more desperate every year.

✤

How dreary someone else's spiritual heroism can be.

✤

Nietzsche and Whitman my fathers: and yet I cannot worship
power. I hate power: I reject it.

✤

In Heaven I hope to have with me
A rare and curious crew;
After the soul's extremity
Only the coarse will do . . .

✤

I have two fathers in eternity:
And each called out of stone the living tree:
The one, a thin-lipped Hun,
And that Irishman
Who taught me how to wear a ragged sleeve . . .

# THE TEACHING OF POETRY

## (1954–58)

Teaching is an act of love, a spiritual cohabitation, one of the few sacred relationships left in a crass secular world.

*

About poetry we can only utter half-truths.

*

I come, a fresh initiate from the fast-disappearing, often-scorned, harried cult of intensity . . .

*

The teaching of poetry requires fanaticism.

*

Teaching needs more squirrels, more individuals, more cranks, more fanatics, (but—and this is simply about what really matters—) more brains . . .

*

This is the lazy man's out often: I haven't read it; therefore it does not exist.

*

And then there is the more honest and charitable mentor who regards poetry as a kind of emotional and spiritual wild oats of the young, a phase of adolescence to be passed through quickly—and anything said to shake him out of this emotional orgy is all to the good.

*

Behind that classical façade—by no means entirely imitation, mind you—lives the soul, the crass nature, of a born impresario: his every action, every letter, his every statement comes from an intense desire to be known, to be reminded of, to be different from, to be a curmudgeon—to be—and here I approach the ultimate—a dictator: now this, I insist, is to be resisted with force and fury. Must all experience be strained through that somewhat congested lower colon? Are students, all of them, to be made solely in his image? Does only he hear it? Nonsense . . .

*

One thing, certainly, that makes for better teaching among the embattled academic young—the last, the real American proletariat, someone said—is the opposition of Authority, the entrenched thin-veined toady to the past, to Harvard, to "values" not only outmoded but obscene.

*

They hear nothing, these stone-deaf enemies of life, literature and the pursuit of anything other than increase in salary.

*

Poetry, like God, is the subject of too much conversation by unformed minds.

*

The goose-me-again-daddy student, that nose-picking I-love-me fraternity cretin . . .

*

The Aggressive: these include, alas, those recently discovered by their mother or some addled high school teacher, devoted to what John Ciardi has called the bonnet-and-bluebird school of poetry; or sometimes sweaty earnest types given to hymnwriting.

✤

Once a week, take a day off to be generous-minded.

✤

What happens is between you and the kids and God, and there's no ratio between your performance and your paycheck.

✤

There is, as Hopkins has told us, no royal road to Parnassus: and likewise no one infallible way to teach poetry. I myself am inclined, often, to the eclectic approach: the helter-skelter attack . . .

✤

Don't fall into the fallacy of believing, as many an aging critic does, that the best poetry exists to permit him to show off.

✤

Teach as an old fishing guide takes out a beginner.

✤

I think some of the effectiveness of my teaching is illusory. I am less complex than, say, Auden, know a good deal less, am and can be therefore closer to the young: they are less cowed, less scared, can pick up my simpler and cruder notions more easily; and have a greater sense of progress. Therefore, to them, I am a "better" teacher. Likewise, the matter of caring: I get guilty about not knowing enough and then begin to "care" terribly. The young are always grateful for attention, nearly all of them—even from a fool, which I think I'm not.

✤

Our lives are instruments: a teacher, I exist to save the young time.

✤

And who is this middle-brow maunderer, muttering in the realms of What Matter?
What aged clichés does he foist upon us?

❉

The professor is supposed to know. I am not of that breed.

❉

I'm drunk, I'm drunk, I'm drunk as I can be.
For I am a member of the faculty!

❉

The nuttier the assignment, often, the better the result.

❉

Intuition is one of the classic and great methods of learning.

❉

You can teach or encourage *some* students to write, yes, poetry
who can't write English.

❉

O Lord, may I never want to look good. O Jesus, may I
always read it all: out loud and the very way it should be.
May I never look at the other findings until I have come
to my own true conclusions: May I care for the least of the
young: and become aware of the one poem that each may
have written; may I be aware of what each thing is, delighted
with form, and wary of the false comparison; may I never
use the word "brilliant."

❉

I realize: I don't just want to give a recital: or whatever it
is: I want to give a whole damn course: I've started thinking
about you as a *class*—and mind you, in my terms! I haven't
been teaching, and so my whole impulse is to teach—isn't
that awful?—like the old brewery horse on the sleigh ride . . .

# THESE EXASPERATIONS

## (1954–58)

My love of poetry is a curse: I read far too much of it, I think too much about it; I compare too many minor birds, making microscopic distinctions, instead of staying on the main theme—what man is, what our relation to God is—I worry about being fair to contemporaries; I remember vast amounts of gossip, rubbish.

❖

—My, but you make a lot of distinctions.
—Isn't that what the mind's for?

❖

The sporadic nature of poetry: poetry is hectic by its very nature. More hectic now?

❖

The lyric is very much alive, not dead; but rare, perhaps, like the recently returning and multiplying egret.

❖

Art: to maintain self against the disruptive whole.

❖

Poetry, if it's any good, is exceedingly human and lets any number of cats out of the bag; and that's why it scares people. And one great big cat is good old sex: And on that

    A phallic symbol's a phallic symbol
    And don't try saying it's mother's thimble . . .

❖

Some poets hate talking; just as tramps hate taking baths.

❖

I suspect to enjoy poetry one ought to compare it with rape.

❖

Some poets are like those fighters badly handled, or never instructed, who get by for a time by virtue of great natural talent but in the end defeat themselves by repeating.

❖

When we begin to misuse gifts—then hell and distortion set in; alas for that poet whom you can read—it's all pretty good, but not quite good enough.

❖

To settle early into multiform:
Life settles in itself: the kitchen bends
The cook; the toy the child; the bosky wood
Intrigues the scrubby marmoset to stay.
Old poets hate their poems, and themselves . . .

❖

It's wiser being good than bad,
It's safer being meek than fierce,
It's fitter being sane than mad—
Say those whose poetry is verse.

❖

He quotes the tougher poets, and talks tough;
But hear his rhythms, fustian huff and puff.

❖

To make me aware of what a mistress of mezzanine kitsch she was, what a self-pitying spiritual fraud, always whining about how tough it is to be a woman—that dreary pitch that seems to be the chief theme of some of our contemporary Sapphos.

✤

The half-prostrate devotee practicing a few choice austerities and perversions in the lap of a hill.

✤

Egomania is the great occupational hazard of the poet today. Some of the most distinguished are among the gravest sinners. You may select your own candidates.

✤

The literary ego is one of the most delicate mechanisms known to man.

✤

Poetry: the supreme test of the critic; so he often is afraid to face it.

✤

He approaches the imagination with the fine delicate touch of a mortician's assistant.

✤

Critics want to talk about what one should know instinctively.

✤

Some critics in announcing that a writer has been "influenced" act as if he has been apprehended rifling the church poor box.

✤

Who think in symbols, naturally, as the mad do, as children do, have a hard time with those fierce sweaty tin-eared logicians who bring to the work of the imagination all the sensibility of a shoe-clerk. But it's in this area that progress must be made. To them there's no logic of the imagination, no place for the suddenly right mad irrelevance, no time or reason for the mind to stretch loose and shrink: no time, in a word, for poetry, an art they pay lip-service to (provided it is in the past).

✳

*Invective on Critics—the Old Lady Loses Her Control Altogether*
—Where's the care for it? The true knowledge of small forms; the fierce fidelity to what is? Not here. These demi-men, these paltry scratchers and fumblers at their own small sores, these linty navel-scrapers, always asking themselves, Do I look all right now? Suppose a major potato comes their way, a hot pistola, a true-blue son of old mother hullabaloo? What do they do? Play Dead like Mr. Shedd. Scribble on the margin "Good for Shedd." The ward-heelers of slightly better minds, grinding and filing away for some piddling piece of provincial podunkus.

✳

I like ambitious people. They're rarely intelligent.

✳

It's these furtive stealers, these feeble fumblers that undo us . . . Some are poor thieves indeed. Their nothing is my world.

✳

American classicists: as if the effort to be austere has left them exhausted: they are tough and hard and not much else, like a lot of tired and dried-up golf balls.

✳

They wear a mask of humility—and then write poems about religious experience which are gross monuments of spiritual pride, presumptuous puling and pawing over what has been directly revealed to better men.

✳

The enemy of great art is vanity: is self-hood, self-hood in the most gruesome forms.

❅

I want to make like Police Commissioner Winters. You know: tough, hard, cryptic. Thump along in simple staves. Boom. Gascoigne. Bump. Jonson. Humph. Dr. Johnson. Tough, hard, spare, sinewy—get it? A few sparse poems, correctly spaced . . . Let me huff and puff a little—the true moral fervor, the high indignant, the rip-rap, red-hot Stanford patented probity—Old Nobody Else Hears It But You.

❅

Guesses about Eliot: As a moral man, he just makes it.
As a mystic, he don't get even to the fringe.
As a literary politician, he has raised politics to statesmanship.

❅

Allusive poetry: it gives those without sensibility something to do.

❅

The distillate of that experience is a faint perfume indeed.

❅

If there's anything new to be said about the Romantics, it will probably come from a yet unappointed Poet Laureate of the Liberian Republic. Haven't we, actually, exhausted ourselves, even granting that each generation must re-evaluate the past?

❅

Crane's assumption: the machine is important; we must put it in our lives, make it part of our imaginative life. Answer: the hell it is. An ode to an icebox is possible, since it contains fruit and meat.

❋

That William Yeats could cover up his mind:
He saw great virtues in a gross behind:
He taught his body to respect a lady;
The lady laughed when she looked at his body;
His head was beautiful: and he would sit
Looking upon whatever mirrored it.
He looked so long upon those greasy mirrors,
That he thought truth spoke only in man's errors.

❋

An American: Something we may recover—a primal nervous-
        ness.
        Perhaps our only important invention is the
        concept of the goodguy.

❋

What a frail but persistent weapon civilization is: how fragile
the handful of concepts: yet tough as wire.

❋

Democracy: where the semi-literate make laws and the il-
literate enforce them.

❋

After Mr. Richard M. Nixon, I feel that sincerity is no longer
possible as a public attitude.

❋

That there are intense spiritual men in America as well as
the trimmers, time-servers, cliché-masters, high-grade mediocrities . . .

❋

Scarcely noble, these exasperations. We forgive the errors of
reason, but not the mistakes of sensibility.

✣

Jesus, don't you ever get worn out with all those bogus aggressions? Don't you know what all these vulgar fulminations mean? You've got more than one papa, and you love them all . . . Don't you buy their books and wear them out? Don't you require them as texts for the young and defend them hotly against the adolescent sneer, the irrelevant footnote, the jackass commentary?

✣

Can he really, can he? Cummings can . . . Could we have the whole heart please? I want all of this man, better than his mask, brighter than his flowers, blithe as his loved mother, more ferocious than his religious father, a friend to ants, joints, joiks, fakes, bowery bums, fruits on the trees and in the trees, the last-best purveyor of compassion we have: a rinky-tink tinkler of shy rarely-played tunes, a watcher of birds and a clear-eyed one at the other end of the telescope pointed straight at the true heaven of Harry's Bar; jumpin jimminy his salvos to Save; holy gee what hasn't he said correctly and sweetly anent holy Joe Gould, a true Harvard hero.

What's better than this bust-a-gut bumping, humping?

Who shez he's sentimental? He shed sho what, you shuddery kid from the last-worst accomedy of wrong answers, what a job they haven't done bedunging the fierce young with their faint furore, their fine wormy windings, up and down, in and out of the bindings, as Burns once said.

Why this guy could do dibble-dab with a dornick. He's always no more than a stone's throw from a true bone, right where it is, he hits me where I used to live and where I am now . . .

Why hell, he even *looks* like my father, who could shoot straight and never bothered to spit except over a high fence. Such precocity in parents is often a burden, mind you, and it's no fair fearing Fearing who hears it too when the subway whams blimety-blam out of the harsh howling holes. Ain't he the frigidaire's friend? . . . . And he's a fairly fast freddie with the fine-honed shiv of sarcasm, wouldn't you say? . . .

Sing, swing, swank, prink, and parade in your languag-wide-swangwhige, bub; but from now on I want you to come straight at the bull. The pure pass when the long horns are right under your tingly bent rusty-dusty right arm. You're no one for being afraid and suppose you do get thrown on your Erse. How's for cutting a few more of the tall trees and making more clearings in the deep woods of the oblivion that crowds down over us all. But sideways, Edward my Estlin, old true marvellous oaf in a shite-poke's clothing, with the pure axe of the Anglo-Saxe o phone music, to hell with all those tired tears from the Tremendous Twenties, leave that to dear old Scotty . . . Jonson and Donne's what you should be like from now on. Otherwise, don't be surprised if some of the fierce young don't steal away or just leave you alone . . .

❋

Better to take an attitude of mind—a stance: thus, while Hardy may have been Auden's father, he learned from the parent to look down from a high vantage point, to see the whole panorama of folly.

❋

As a provincial, an American, no fool, I hope, but an ignoramus, I believe we need Europe—more than she needs us: the Europe of Char, of Perse, of Malraux, of Michaux, those living men with their sense of history, of what a free man is . . .

❋

I slid into Victor Hugo's home as silently as a slug.

# A PSYCHIC JANITOR

## (1959–63)

As a critic, I am no more than a janitor, a psychic janitor
cleaning up what others have left sorting through—could it be
some beautiful poem, or rubbish?

*

I don't care what a writer claims, or what, even, he talks
about—even if the talk is good—that's for the discursive, albeit
organized mind, for academia, for the lecturer, for the logic-
choppers, the whereto and why boys. This is all second-order
creation of reality. Poetry is, first, last, and foremost creation,
the supreme creation, for me, at least in language . . . I'm
sick of fumbling, furtive, disorganized minds like bad lawyers
trying to make too many points that *this* is an age of criticism:
and these, mind you, tin-eared punks who couldn't tell a poem
from an old boot if a gun were put to their heads. These
jerks who know twelve lines of Dante, the early Tiresome
Tom, and Ezra Pound's laundry notes. These are the most
monstrous, pretentious arbiters that yet appeared on the academic scene.

*

There's another typical stance: only *I* hear it. Then just listen:
hump, schlump, bump—half the time: a real—did I say real?
—I mean *unreal*, unnatural—thumping away in stupid staves,
an arbitrary lopping of lines, rhythms, areas of experience, a
turning away from much of life, an exalting of a few limited
areas of human consciousness. All right, I say, make like that,
and die in your own way: in other words limited, provincial,

classical in a distorted and—I use the word carefully—degraded sense; "American" in the sense American means eccentric, warped, and confined.

I am fed up with some of the poems of self-congratulation by our poetic elders, that *I have lived a life of self-control* sort of thing, that gruesome spiritual smugness that comes from being ever so talky with and about God—God, Job, and the Lord Jesus himself. There's no doubt, once we are aware of, once we venture into the area of the spiritual all dangers increase—there's always spiritual pride, that greatest of sins . . .

There's more than one variety of disease in this area of experience: the tiny epiphany, the cozy moment in the suburban rose garden, the ever so slight shimmer in the face of afternoon reality—not much more than the Georgians seemed to be talking about . . .

\*

A lot of tired beetles, these American classicists. It's as if the effort to be austere has left them with nothing much else than the impulse to congratulate themselves on being something else than their contemporaries—small-fry Hemingways who have read Homer.

\*

I'm aware that among the expert (unfrightened) trans-Atlantic literary theologians to approach God without benefit of clergy is a grievous lapse in taste, if not a mortal sin. But in crawling out of a swamp, or up what small rock-faces I try to essay, I don't need a system on my back.

\*

Two Retorts to Eliot

I

Our God Himself adores
Only *beasts* upon all fours:
Humility's for bores.

II

What do we need to foil intolerable Fate?
A God we kiss to, standing on our feet.

*

Essay: I Hate Eliot
1st sentence. Why?
Because I love him too much—

*

The pseudo-poem; the whipped-up poem; the "decoration," the
intimacies of bogus and shoddy love affairs; the insights acquired running between the boudoir and the altar; rewritten
St. Theresa and St. Catherine.

*

What poetry may need at this point is a *certain* vulgarity, not
*all* vulgarities. What Synge referred to: the brutality, in a word,
the aliveness of life.

*

What's *important*? That which is dug out of books, or out of
the guts? What's important? Lacerations, whipped-up accusations
interlarded schoolboy Latin quotations or the language really
modified, a new rhythm . . . ?

*

If we muddle and thump through a paraphrase, with side
comments, however brilliant, we still do not have the poem.

*

For the poem—even the fairly good poem—means an entity, a
unity has been achieved that transcends by far the organization
of the lecture, the essay, even the great speech. This the
academics at least should know—and more and more of them
do. They were put on the world to understand this: it's high
time some of them did.

*

We cry against critics: because it's so important they be better.

\*

I think poetic experience in the modern world must, of necessity, be primarily concerned with depth rather than breadth. A Goethe is no longer possible; but an intense personal poetry . . .

\*

I've always found Robert Frost's remark about free verse—he'd rather play tennis with the net down—I've always found this wonderfully suggestive, as an old coach, in a great number of ways. For one thing I coached at Penn State. We played in clothing cast off—laundered of course—by the football team. Of course, my derriere being what it is, I frequently found not only the net at least semi-down, but also my pants . . . You know how things get from too much laundering: the rubber in the various intimate equipment disintegrates, the string would bust in my sweat pants: there'd be a hole in my racket. Well, do you get the analogy: that's me and free verse. Frost, he had a racket and balls all his life; but some of us out in the provinces operated under difficulties: we've had our disorganized lives and consequently our intractable material: we've had to use free verse, on occasion.

\*

I never could understand the objection to "free" verse—it's only bad, i.e. slack, lax, sloppy free verse one objects to. For the net, in final terms, is stretched even tighter. Since the poet has neither stanza form nor rhyme to rely on, he has to be more cunning than ever, in manipulating, modulating his sounds, and keeping that forward propulsion, and making it all natural. Instead of end-rhyme, of course, he has internal rhyme, assonance, consonance. But he can't fall back on tradition as much as a formalist. It's the pause, the natural pause that matters, Lawrence said somewhere—said it better, of course. He has to depend more on his own ear.

We seem to be shyer of the prose-poem than the French. Maybe it fits their language better . . . I rather think this: that the modern poet can afford to get closer to prose much more easily and profitably and less dangerously than the writer of prose can afford to be "poetic." I think of how spongy, how ersatz some of those passages from Virginia Woolf are . . .

Let's say it's another kind of thing, maybe a lesser thing, the settable song, but let's also admit that it is enormously difficult to do. After all there was Shakespeare, and Campion, and even the Joyce of *Chamber Music.* And there are those who think Yeats' plays were mere settings to the songs within them . . . It depends on the very energy of the psyche, the inner ear. The Victorians, many of them, were tired, and they wrote a tired poetry, though often subtle rhythmically. *"I am half-sick of shadows," said the Lady of Shalott.* She didn't have the spiritual guts to peer into the black, to take a full look at the worst.

It became a whole psychological stance which Yeats himself picks up in his youth: the tired young man on the sofa; today we have the tired young man in the gutter.

Understand I'm not making a cult of violent energy in itself. One is often offended, for instance, by Browning's huffing and puffing, let's-have-no-nonsense sort of thing; and some of the bouncy ballads of Chesterton and the other English ballad-ists I can't abide; or the heavy swats that Housman sometimes will use in his ballad metres. But let's hasten to say that Housman can modulate beautifully . . .

As our poetry has become increasingly dramatic, in the sense it often represents a struggle or a dialogue between our selves (didn't Yeats say we make of our quarrels with others, rhetoric; of our quarrels with ourselves, poetry?): and with these poems becoming longer, often representing the protago-nist under considerable stress, poets have had to learn to write a poetry that follows the motion of the mind itself: hence some of the associational jumps, the shifts, in subject matter and rhythm, the changes in speed. That is, the poet does not merely talk, or ruminate, he cries out in turn, in agony, in rage. This puts enormous demands on the writer: it is as if he is writing the high scenes in a tragic drama. And his shifts, his jumps, his changes of pace have to be imaginatively right, or all is lost; it will be a nothing, a windy bombast. We seem to demand or want a poetry with the personality under great stress.

❊

The human mind, in the desperate effort to be gay, has produced so little *real* nonsense, so few funny poems, so few poems of joy.

❊

R.F., W.C.W.
The Muse taught them a way of being plain,
Who, like the sun, grew greater going down.

❊

In Muir, I find an almost intolerable sense of the sadness of existence.

❊

Wilbur: can look at a thing, and talk about it beautifully, can turn it over in his mind, and draw truths from a scene, easily and effortlessly (it would seem)—though his kind of writing requires the hardest kind of discipline, it must be remembered. Not a graceful mind—that's a mistake—but a mind of grace, an altogether different and higher thing.

❊

Let the uncharitable, the obtuse say all they will, bringing their charges—sentimentality; of using words (*flower*) as counters; of creating ambiguous non-states of being; of sniggering; of posturing . . . ethical self-indulgence; of failing to change after the first two books . . . of arbitrary syntactical nuttiness;—yet Cummings always remains a throwback if you will, but a throwback to something truly wonderful, almost lost from the language: the secret of being lyrically funny, the secret of being truly alive and happy. He has revived, renewed more than we know. All right, he's father-haunted. Who isn't? He'd be a monster if he were otherwise . . .

I think of Cummings, not as a poet of one kind of thing, one genre, one singularity, but as one who has explored various and important and often neglected sides of modern sensibility:

1. The child's. Here, it seems to me, he moves within the mind of the child, *is* the child, if you will—without condescending or being coy—an enormously difficult feat.

2. The adolescent's. And this area of experience is a real trap, with the reader so often conditioned by the notion that the young don't really suffer. They're just oversize children with stock reactions, living out the misadventures of inexperience, uttering only stylized lingo, boring as advertising formulae.

There are these randy various jumpings, a many-faceted marvellous man.

He is not content to doodle along in the five-foot line.

In an age of cozy-toe operators, he has always been ready to take a chance . . .

❉

Put it this way: I detest dogs, but adore wolves.

❉

I'm beginning to think like a novelist. Is that death?

❉

How crude, how irrelevant those reports of reality called fiction! The worst honest poems are better. Who cares that Arnold Bennett ever lived? Or even Huxley?

❉

Fitzgerald: He was born, and died, a Princeton sophomore. (A Princeton sophomore was cute; we, at least, were sinister. We didn't play at being gangsters, we were gangsters.)

❋

If I could but respect prose!—would I be happy?

❋

In poetry, there are no casual readers.

❋

My hope younger than I, of course,
Disdains Yeatsian remorse;
That balm of academic wits,
And sophomoric sugar-tits.
Remorse for what?

❋

The imagist poet: runs out of objects, his eye tires.

❋

Perhaps the poet's path is closer to the mystic than we think:
his thought becomes more imageless.

❋

The body of imagery, possibly, thins out or purifies itself or
the mind moves into a more abstract mode, closer to wisdom,
in talent of a high order.

❋

Those without poetry: their source of innocence lost.

❋

"But reading poetry is as natural an activity as eating one's
breakfast." Alas, some people associate it with other natural
functions.

❋

People can and do understand poetry but they don't want to:
it is a danger.

❋

O Muse, when shall I arrive at a true sense of history,
I who have served pre-history so long and well?

❋

An eager young coed was poised with her pencil. What is the most interesting phenomenon in American poetry, Mr. Roethke? What I do next, he said, abandoning her for a ham sandwich. My Gaad, he's rude, she said. No, he's just hungry. His tapeworm just had a nervous breakdown.

❋

Anonymous is my favorite author.

# THE BEAUTIFUL DISORDER

(1954–63)

So it's to begin by beginning, and what words I have won't bring you to love—for the language of this life. It's you I mean, already in a half-drowse of stale fancies, absurd notions of meter, muddy welters of unbeautiful thoughts, the turgid lyrics of adolescence. For it's one of the muddiest times of all—worse than senility, in some ways, for Grandma at least remembers, and has said and thought her dreary little tags so often that they have a finish and a rhythm . . .

Roaring asses, hysterics, I invoke you. I ask your unquiet aid in this collective dismembering and dissemination of wits . . .

✳

We can't escape what we are, and I'm afraid many of my notions about verse (I haven't too many) have been conditioned by the fact that for nearly 25 years I've been trying to teach the young something about the nature of verse by writing it—and that with very little formal knowledge of the subject or previous instruction. So it's going to be like Harpo Marx teaching the harp.

✳

My doctor says I have fantasies of omnipotence about teaching: that I can teach any idiot, in the course of three quarters, to write at least one piece of verse that an intelligent man can read with pleasure.

✻

Those students get the highest grades who take their responsibilities of educating me most seriously.

✻

I have only a few ideas; and some of them are almost dead from overwork . . .

✻

I think at least we have this distinction: the Russians, up to now, haven't claimed to have invented "Creative Writing." Frankly, as far as I'm concerned, they're welcome to it.

✻

. . . In part you accept what "I" know: but I also am most anxious to find out what *you* know, care about, like, listen to, are moved by: no one hears everything; even the greatest can make absurd errors in judgment—particularly with reference to contemporaries. Goethe and Schiller let Hölderlin pass by under their noses, but the really good ones, the intense passionate ones, had their contemporaries sized up: look at Hopkins on Browning, on Wordsworth; think how acute Keats was in sensing the odious pomposity in Wordsworth. The wonder of wonders is the unanimity of judgment among practicing writers . . .

Before you are wild, you first have to be, not tame, but capable of being contained; or containing yourself, your psyche: that which is stored up.

So, and I admit that to an extent I set myself up as an arbiter, think of me as a spy from outside who has come back with good news . . .

✻

I expect you to be human beings. Don't laugh—that's already an incredible assumption: they're a disappearing species.

✻

Remember nestlings: I'm here to see you live.

*

I'm paid to remind you what you are.

*

Poetry-writing (the craft) can't be taught, but it can be insinuated.

*

Not inspiration but the breaking down of strong habitual barriers.

*

There are only a few little secrets. If I give them to you all at once, you would be addled. For each truth has its stage.

*

Make ready for your gifts. Prepare. Prepare.

*

Our problem is to get something done, to get started somewhere, away from the rubbish of our respective corners, out of coma or confusion toward some crack of the light, some piece of what really is.

*

Allow me a certain sententiousness, since this comes from a desire to have you avoid my own mistakes.

*

But let me say what I'm up to.

1st, To point out a few of the elements, structural or otherwise, which seem to make for the memorable, particularly striking lines.

2nd, To show how texture affects rhythm, particularly in the song-like poem.

3rd, To indicate a few of the strategies open to the writer of the irregular prose-like poem.

❋

There's one kind of prose-poem which is simply provided by the succession of events. This can be enormously hard to do—and not destroy the emphasis by blowing the material beyond what it is, becoming portentous or just plain dull . . . The nature of the subject can provide, can be the expediency: when the thing is seen long enough, observed intensely enough, if one is sufficiently involved emotionally, the details dribble out. The poem takes a kind of natural shape.

❋

You will live, at times, to curse your sense of form: How much easier it is to sprawl all over, to be a mere receiver . . .

❋

Form acts the father: tells you what you may and may not do.

❋

A writer can get trapped in a form, in a psychological stance, an attitude, and he must struggle, often, to extricate himself or he may die . . .

❋

Any form, even those great ones hallowed by tradition, can become a trap.

❋

The sonnet: a great form to pick your nose in.

❋

A more objective and more oblique art depends less upon the language itself, is less likely to be defiled or worn by time.

❋

One does not become another poet by simply adoring him, by making him a psychic pin-up boy.

✳

Someone said you have been influenced? Indeed, and no doubt you also drank your mother's milk.

✳

Advice to the young: don't fret too much about being "influenced," but make sure you chew up your old boy with a vengeance, blood, guts and all.

✳

For poetry, my dear, is not
Things other people said & thought
    Nor what you're thinking.

✳

I want you to rise above Spokane!

✳

It's hard work, and you won't want it for long. Never mind being a mad poet; just concentrate on being a poet, for the time being. And it's not true, as Freud or some other mythologist has said, that everyone can write nonsense.

✳

Don't try to refine your singularities all at once. Don't work too hard at being nutty—you may make it all too soon, our culture being what it is.

✳

One trouble is of course . . . that the poet in mid-career, as I may say, or should it be male menopause—all his masks begin to disappear or he begins to disappear before all his masks: the roaring boy, the bully of the campus, the beast of Bennington, the raping tinker of Chenango Valley.

✳

I confess to a certain fondness for these poems: perhaps they have, like some bastards, the charm of a community effort.

✤

A defective rhythmic sense which comes from wrenching language into a pattern almost a poem (related to prose sensibility). The management of the syllable is the very core of the problem: I think it is related to the question of articulation itself: the voice box . . .

✤

Phase 37: That every damn thing one does is a manifestation of genius.

✤

I'm the genius of the world, of that there is no doubt.
Said Epictetus to the foetus, Does your mother know you're out?

✤

The young poet feels in himself powers which are far from being expressed: he wishes to be honored for his impulse, not the performance.

✤

The greatest assassin of life is haste.

✤

There can be not-work of great emotional charge: necessary to the growth of the soul and to one's technical advancement (Are they so different?).

✤

There is a point in the slow progress to maturity when thinking about oneself becomes no longer a major pleasure . . .

✤

Leave "truths" to your elders, and take on the burden of observation.

✤

Nothing seen, nothing said.

✵

Not only to perceive the single thing sharply: but to perceive
the relationships between many things sharply perceived.

✵

A figure is a judgment, so they say;
The mind can never take a holiday:
It's not the pure irrational we know:
The forebrain likes its children to be slow.

✵

I think we could do with more style, more assonance, more
elan, more verve, more animal spirits, more *fun*. These are not
solemn matters.

✵

The comic—the really funny before the eye of God—is harder
to achieve than the lyric; more anguishing, more exacting, more
exhausting to its writer.

✵

Variation: there's a technical problem: when to rest. But it
need not bother you who rest so easy.

✵

Rare the writer who knows what his material really is, particularly the young writer.

✵

The point comes when any honest writer will come to realize he
is done with a particular body of material: that henceforward
everything in that vein may be eminently respectable, perhaps
even better than anyone else could do—but none the less a
little less good, the edge not quite so sharp, and this point
should be recognized early.

❋

Bring to poetry the passion that goes into politics or buying a piece of meat.

❋

I recommend that you go, on your own, and immediately, to poets closer to your own age. Some may reflect your own confusions—let them be nameless—read *them* passionately *and* critically.

❋

To enter the mind of his contemporaries—that surely is one of the tasks of the artist.

❋

I don't say, Come off it: I say stay with it, come on it, do it *grosser* and greater, larger and fatter, earlier and later.

❋

Energy is the soul of poetry. Explosive active language.

❋

Artist's problem: to get to the best in one's self. And then get away from it.

❋

The difficulty comes, at times, from the loss of perspective. There's no great harm in being somebody else once in a while. There you will come to know how, by working slowly, to be spontaneous.
To bring the poem to what it should be and no more.
Such interior meltings, sighs, outcries of ravishment, rose-blown, fly-blown fantasies.
Yet some thefts are reprehensible; this is what is worrying you . . .

✣

The crimes: wasting technical skill on a trivial theme; being idiotically addicted to form, stanza form; doodling with dead diction.

✣

There's a point where plainness is no longer a virtue, when it becomes excessively bald, wrenched.

✣

The literal—that grave of all the dull.

✣

It's the shifting of the thought that's important, often—the rightness (or wrongness!) of the imaginative jump. Many modern poets still are content only with the logical progression, or with metaphors—often beautiful, elaborate, fresh—but these consisting of little more than a listing of appositives. In the richest poetry even the juxtaposition of objects should be pleasurable; hence, Neruda, even in indifferent translation, is pleasurable.

✣

To make the line in itself interesting, syntactically, that is the problem.

✣

A paradox: more know what a poem is than what a line is . . .

✣

A many-sided man has many rhythms.

✣

We have forgotten the importance of the list. We have the better surrealists to remind us.

✣

All great breaks in consciousness or styles are very simple; but enormously important.

✢

It is the mark of the true poet that he perpetually renews himself.

✢

"I've learned a lot in this course. I don't understand a thing you say, but I just watch your hands." Hardly a tribute to one's verbal powers.

✢

I had eaten the apple ere you were weaned. I bring the derision of walls, enchantress sure of your body, extremest oriole. What little you have shown me, I love—like my own first fat-fingered effusion . . .

✢

I don't care if you crawled on your knees from Timbuctoo: and think me the greatest thing since the living Buddha: I'll not, no I'll not nurse you, etc. Every poet must be, has to be, remembah: his *own* mother . . .

✢

The poem, even a short time after being written, seems no miracle; unwritten, it seems something beyond the capacity of the gods.

✢

The thing conceived; the thing finally said—a vast distance.

✢

Every sentence a cast into the dark.

✢

What is hard to endure—the peculiar and haunting sense that one is about to write a poem, and then have no poem come; or be interrupted by trivia, by fools, by sense.

✢

You must believe: a poem is a holy thing—a good poem, that is.

*

Remind yourself once more of the absolute holiness of your task.

*

To write poetry: you have to be prepared to die.

*

A schoolmaster should *not* like to keep his disciples.

*

Create: then disown.

*

You've led me to more than I am.
O lead me on, brief children,
To those white regions where no soul is spoiled.

*

I am overwhelmed by the beautiful disorder of poetry, the eternal virginity of words.